Stop The World . . . Our Gerbils Are Loose!

Stop The World...
Our Gerbils Are Loose!

*Ann Toland Serb
and Joan Wester Anderson*

1979
DOUBLEDAY & COMPANY, INC.
GARDEN CITY, NEW YORK

Grateful acknowledgment is made to the following:

To *Marriage and Family Living* (a division of Abbey Press) for "The Impossible Athlete," "Remember the Rose!" "Count-down to Party-Time," "Spring Do-It-Yourself-Itis" (herein titled "The Anderson Cover-up"), and "The Good Ole Summertime." Copyright © 1977, 1976, 1976, 1977, 1977, respectively, by Marriage and Family Living. Reprinted by permission of the publisher.
To *Catholic Digest* for "Beware the Ides of April," which appeared in the April 1978 issue. Copyright © 1978 by the College of St. Thomas, and reprinted with the permission of the Catholic Digest.

"A Kiss for Kindergarten" originally appeared in *Family Digest Parish Monthly*. Copyright © 1975 by Our Sunday Visitor, Inc.
"Confessions of a Contented Woman" originally appeared in *Our Sunday Visitor*. Copyright © 1975 by Our Sunday Visitor, Inc.

Library of Congress Cataloging in Publication Data

Serb, Ann Toland.
    Stop the world . . . our gerbils are loose.

    1. Housewives—United States. 2. Family—
United States.   I. Anderson, Joan Wester.
II. Title.
HQ536.S45   301.42′7
ISBN: 0-385-14509-8
Library of Congress Catalog Card Number: 78-62605

To Ann and Joe Toland,
   Monica and Ted Wester,
   the irreplaceable grandparents
   who have encouraged the exploits of
   Tom, Mary, Ann, Joe, Bob, Steve, Chris, and Bill Serb,
   Chris, Tim, Bill, Brian, and Nancy Anderson
   as a form of long-delayed heavenly justice.

Contents

CONTENTS

Stop The World . . . Our Gerbils Are Loose!

Introduction:
The Start of Something New

It began innocently enough one wintry day, when the snow piled up softly outside the house and my spirits plummeted within. Hip-deep in preschoolers, I welcomed the ring of the telephone with all the enthusiasm a dying-of-thirst desert traveler might display toward a frosty pitcher of lemonade.

"I've had the most fantastic idea!" announced my friend Joan over the suburb-to-city lifeline of housebound mothers. "It will cure our doldrums, expand our horizons, bolster our egos, and trim our waistlines!"

"Send me two cases of whatever it is!" I pleaded, tripping over the Monopoly game, two costumes that had to be hemmed for the third act of the teen show, and a papier-mâché reconstruction of Mount Everest. "Between the weather, the kids, the ironing—which, by the way, I still haven't gotten around to doing—and all the home-baked goodies I'm using to keep this mob quiet, I'm really desperate. I'll buy or do *anything* for a change of pace."

Stopping only long enough to scoop up somebody small who walked past me carrying his father's electric razor and headed in the general direction of the hamster, I got back to Joan.

"Tell me your fantastic idea," I begged, reaching over to confiscate the last loaf of bread and a jar of honey as they strolled by.

"Well," she said, stopping only long enough to scoop up somebody small who was throwing orange peels all over her kitchen, "we're going to write a book!"

"You're crazy!" I informed my friend, stopping only long enough to check out the latest crash in my pantry. "Why don't we try something easy, like brain surgery or macramé?"

"You said we're a pair of modern, well-organized, talented women," she reminded me, ignoring a crash in her pantry.

"I meant whipping up something for the bake sale and running the car pool," I explained, confiscating a bowl of goldfish being carried past me in the general direction of the toilet.

"You said we can do anything we put our minds to," she insisted, fielding a gerbil that flew by her.

"I meant matching up all the socks as they come out of the drier and trying that new recipe for quiche Lorraine," I explained, stopping only long enough to deliver another puppy under the table.

There was a slight pause while she confiscated a cat being carried past her in the general direction of the washing machine.

"Look," she reminded me, "it's going to be a long, cold winter. What did you have planned?"

I mentally ran over my list. There was the ironing basket, the bottom of which I hadn't seen since 1969. Then there were the closets, the back of which I might not see before 1989. And the diaper pail, the last of which I hoped to see sometime in 1979. But other than that . . .

"Nothing," I told her honestly.

"Well then, we'll write the book. Together. The two of us."

"Just one problem," I pointed out, reaching to catch a two-year-old swinging from the kitchen light fixture. "What will we write about? Nothing ever happens around here."

Never being a pair of women to crumple before small obstacles, we didn't let that stop us. But the reaction of one spouse nearly put the kiss of death on the entire project.

"Joan and I are going to write a book," I informed my husband at supper, then dashed for instructions on reviving someone who had just inhaled an entire pork chop in one gasp. When he recovered, he returned to the subject at hand.

"YOU and WHO are going to WHAT?" he wheezed, torn between suffocation and fits of laughter. "This I've got to see. Just how can you work with a partner who actually cleans her refrigerator and knows where the umbrella is, when you can't even find the vacuum? Well, as I said, this I've got to see!"

For once in his life, he might have been right. There was Joan, running a well-oiled family operation in the suburbs in spite of five children (four sons and a darling little daughter) and a husband who often came home for lunch. (Other than that, he's practically perfect.) And here was I, trying to hang in there amid the confusion of my city domain, complete with eight children (six sons and two darling teen daughters) and a husband who often made snide remarks. (Other than that, he's practically perfect.) Joan, on a slow day, can wallpaper and regrout her bathroom before breakfast, while I on a good day . . . but enough.

It's some consolation to know that Joan sends all her mending to her mother, while I, after every sale on sheets, whip up magnificent slipcovers and drapes to add a festive touch to rooms that otherwise resemble the inside of a gorilla cage. And when I occasionally describe the joys of home-baked bread to her, she goes into cardiac arrest.

Long ago we decided that, should God melt us down and try again, He might bring forth two perfect people. Both would have veins flowing with Joan's organization, yet retain my ability to "ho-hum" my way through an entire semester of costume-making and failure slips.

My husband, of course, could never understand the desperate lengths to which two totally incompatible women will go when faced with a winter of isolation shared by pint-sized playmates. We welcomed sessions at our typewriters as a golden opportunity to make some noise of our own for a change. January, February, and March whizzed past, sped along by frequent phone consultations.

"Now let's see," Joan read from her checklist. (She was in charge of organization, since I was still trying to locate the desk.) "If you tackle toilet training, Cub Scouts, and entertaining . . ."

". . . And you whip up pieces on money, politics, and gardening . . ."

"Gardening?" she asked, rescuing a guinea pig being carried in the general direction of the hair drier.

"Gardening," I said firmly. "The thing your neighbors do all summer when you're indoors waxing the bathtub. Seeds. Fertilizer. Rose plants. That sort of thing."

"Maybe I could get a book out of the library," she sighed doubtfully, "and have the kindergartner explain it all to me. . . ."

"Would you rather do something on cooking?" I suggested sarcastically, "or sewing, or . . ."

"I'll get you something on gardening," she promised, aware that I was only too familiar with her Achilles' heels, as she was with mine. "But no cooking, or you'll have to do the bit on housework."

"Agreed," I said, recognizing a good deal when it's thrust before me.

Somehow or other, since miracles still happen, our winter madness turned into the summer reality of a completed manuscript—which I promptly plopped before he of little faith.

"We did it. What have you got to say now?" I asked smugly, serving up a large helping of crow and daring him to request seconds.

"Writing the book was the easy part," he insisted. "Now comes the hard one. You have to find a publisher."

He had little to offer in the line of additional commentary, however, since he was busy excavating the ironing basket in his perpetual search for handkerchiefs. So Joan and I, knowing nothing about the difficulties involved in finding a publisher, located one immediately. Some months later (about as many as it takes to produce a real baby), we held the first copies of our joint child tenderly in our hands.

"*Love, Lollipops and Laundry,*" I murmured reverently. "It does have a certain ring to it."

16

"Who said two women with thirteen children can do anything they want?" Joan cheered, plucking a two-year-old off her ankles.

"You did," I admitted, grabbing a bowl of corn flakes being carried past me in the general direction of the electric fan. "I'm still trying to find the vacuum cleaner."

"And who said this is only the first of many?" she triumphed, hauling a toddler out of the dishwasher.

"You did," I confirmed, whacking a hand reaching for the refrigerator. "Personally, I'd like to call it a day on this whole book-writing business. Eight kids ought to be enough of a career for anybody, and I still can't find my desk. It must be buried under the ironing somewhere."

"Next time it's my turn to type," she coaxed, hugging the cat and putting out the three-year-old. "Consider all the raw material delivered daily to your door. Would you want to waste all that pain, that aggravation, that next semester's course in driver's education, that first-grade play, that . . ."

"Enough!" I begged. "How soon would you like to start? According to the weather bureau, it's going to be another long, hard winter. We need something to keep us busy through snow, sleet, and unpressed tablecloths."

And here it is. . . .

Happily Ever After

Anniversary Inventory

JOAN

"Running a house is simply a matter of organization," my husband began pointing out before my bridal bouquet had even withered. As a starry-eyed bride, I could only marvel at this sterling example of male logic. Until I realized that Spouse was expecting me to live up to it.

But what is a woman to do when she spends her girlhood preparing to care for her husband's needs, then discovers shortly after marriage that she can barely cope with her own?

"Here, give me that steak!" Spouse told me indignantly one evening in our honeymoon cottage. "It's already dead—you don't have to kill it!"

"I'm just following the recipe," I protested, smoothing my ruffly apron and trying to look like a professional *Hausfrau*.

"The recipe says 'broil,' not 'boil.' "

"I thought that was a misprint," I told him meekly.

"Why don't you go and dust or something, while I whip up some homemade steak soup?" he snapped.

I've been dusting for seventeen years now. Unfortunately, as I discovered soon after our vow exchange, Husband is better at almost every household chore than I am. His shirt collars stiffen if he merely glances at them while fingering the steam iron. My finished laundry looks as if I haven't started yet. He can shop for a week's worth of groceries without missing an item; I stand in the middle of Frozen Foods, trying to remember if we're out of cream cheese or Cream of Wheat. Or maybe crème de menthe. When he vacuums, the throw rugs shudder for a week afterward. When I clean, our dust balls curl up for a nice long nap under the couch, in no danger of being disturbed.

Part of our problem is that Spouse and I differ on what is really important in life. Years ago I did try to maintain a Superwife status—disinfecting the oven light bulb at regular intervals, spray-polishing the insides of wastebaskets. Until the day I made the discovery that has become my household motto: "Dirt Returns."

Since that time I have worked up to sloth on a gradual basis—first disposing of all recipes containing more than two ingredients, then painting the bathtub black, and finally letting a house plant die. The feeling of freedom is heady, and I now have time for more meaningful pursuits, such as taking another semester of Decorating with Fossils. Needless to say, Husband is not amused by my value system.

"I'm not asking you to work *hard*," he sighed in bewilderment a few years back, while surveying the cobwebs in my sewing box. "All you really have to do is sit on a kitchen stool and supervise the *kids*. We've produced all this cheap labor—we might as well use it!"

"That's more trouble than it's worth," I retorted. "Frankly, the idea of the baby cooking a spaghetti dinner leaves me cold. . . ."

"Well . . ."

"And do you really think it's a good idea to let the six-year-old wallpaper our hallway? How will he ever build the scaffolding?"

"Well . . ."

Actually, Husband has the right idea—the kids should be directed into maintaining their share of the housework. But since I lack the necessary qualifications for the job of director (I do not possess a black belt in karate, and have never learned hypnosis), I've taken the easy approach: let's all pitch in, do the essentials, and leave the rest to wrinkle, mold, or wither, as the case may be.

If Husband were a chauvinist pig, refusing to pour his own coffee much less brew it, my position would be clear: I could simply thumb my nose at him, while stepping over the mending on my way to a consciousness-raising session. But what recourse does a woman have when her husband willingly turns out stacks of perfect pancakes for Saturday brunch, and then discovers that she forgot to buy syrup? Claiming temporary insanity is no excuse— seventeen years of forgetfulness can hardly be classified as "temporary." Claiming an allergy to pancakes doesn't work either.

Even more humiliating is Spouse's performance when he must run the house during my annual illness breaks. One would assume that a man faced with five children home on a rainy spring vacation, a wife enjoying every luxurious moment of life in Intensive Care, and eleven broken curtain rods (compliments of Boys' Badminton 101) would hitchhike to Vancouver—or at least *tremble* a little. Not on your life.

"Everything's under control at home," my Better Half assured me one day during visiting hours, "especially now that the kids are all sleeping on the highway. I rerouted your car pool—you were wasting a lot of gas—canned some cucumbers, and painted the bedroom today."

"You look tired," I told him hopefully. "Are you sure you're getting enough rest?"

"Never felt better! Running a home is simply a matter . . ."

"Would you ring for the nurse?" I asked him. "I need a pain shot." Hopefully, it would sedate me for the next ten years, or until I discovered what I'm supposed to be doing with my life.

"I wish I had your problem," a neighbor of mine sighed recently. "My Frank doesn't know one end of a diaper from the other. He thinks dinners grow inside of our freezer. Last month I caught him washing the windows with hair spray. You don't know how lucky you are!"

"Maybe," I told her, "but how would you feel if the grade school Fun Fair committee requested that your *husband* donate this year's fudge brownies?"

"You're taking this much too seriously." She lowered her voice.

"We never told you this, but when you had your surgery, Frank and I saw your husband in the yard on two separate occasions, weeping quietly into a sponge."

"Really?"

"And did you know that during the church's Barter Sale, he offered to trade all of your children for a pan of lasagna?"

"You're kidding!" I was beginning to feel better.

She patted my shoulder. "Any husband can outshine his wife if he does her job *occasionally*. But we women are committed on a permanent basis, and it takes real heroism to get up in the morning. Just remember that the next time Mr. Perfection discovers some lint on his socks!"

I wandered into the kitchen where Husband was completing my crossword puzzle.

"Do you feel our life together is relevant and meaningful?" I asked.

He looked up suspiciously. "Have you enrolled in another of those psychology courses?"

"No, I'm serious. Why on earth did you marry *me*?"

He abandoned his word search for a three-toed sloth, stood up, and put his arms around me.

"Because I love you," he said.

"A perfectly good reason. . . ."

"Because life with you is usually difficult, but never dull. And because you laugh a lot."

"Actually, that's hysteria," I told him. "But thank you for letting me know."

"Suppose you let me know," Husband asked, "what we're having for dinner tonight."

"Homemade steak soup. I misread the recipe again."

Quite frankly, it's been an interesting seventeen years. I can hardly wait to see what happens next.

Making Cents of the
Family Budget

ANN

"Look, dear, we've got to sit down tonight and go over the bills together."

Such words would make any marriage counselor's heart leap with joy. A husband and wife, co-operating and communicating on the battlefield known as family finance! How uplifting! How inspiring!

Before any normal husband and wife sit down to "discuss" the fiscal facts of family life, however, they should agree on two basic principles:

1) There's never enough money.

2) They are about to have one heck of a fight over what little money there is.

Only then is it realistic for them to proceed into the checkbook arena for Round One.

Many years of domestic debate over the finer points of household finance (Should he continue his investment program in vital areas like bowling, three-inch steaks, and poker, or will I continue to squander our fortune on such frivolities as peanut butter, laun-

24

dry detergent, and kids' underwear?) have given Himself and me certain insight into what experts have laughingly termed "discretionary funds."

We now hold the following truths to be self-evident:

a) The "save it for a rainy day" soul always weds a "spend it while it's hot" devotee. Fire and water may not mix, but this particular combination continues to bring a certain zest to dollar discussions.

b) The partner who balances the checkbook is obsessed by those two digits to the right of the decimal point, while the one who habitually *uses* the checkbook has strong moral objections to filling out any little stubs.

This makes awaiting the monthly bank statement a genuine adventure in anticipation—"Will we/won't we be overdrawn this time?" (Each player is entitled to choose the option most compatible with his/her general economic philosophy.) Joint checking accounts are designed to bring life partners into frequent, frantic conversations. It's a good thing, too, or they might stop talking altogether. These sessions also furnish the neighbors with stimulating insights into investment programs or impending bankruptcy, when the weather is warm and the windows are open.

While I sincerely subscribe to Anderson's Law of High (and Low) Family Finance—"Whichever partner handles the money worries about the money"—I've also evolved my own theory. Serb's Economic Principle is best summed up: "All rainy day savings will promptly be swept away by some deluge of disasters not predicted by any newscast weatherperson."

Basic research for this theory was performed some years ago. Himself and I, for the first time in our family history, had accumulated the obstetrician's fee shortly before a baby arrived. (Our usual practice had been to send the kid toddling in, clutching his own post-dated check.) But the week before Child Number Five debuted, our dog was hit by a car. Himself promptly whipped her into the animal hospital, then returned home with the happy news that she could be repaired.

"How much will it cost?" I inquired with the curiosity born

25

from years of struggling over tiny budget projections that crumpled quickly when confronted by a real-life stack of bills.

"Does it matter?" responded the Last of the Big Spenders. (Since he isn't the one who explains to the O.B. why that last payment for delivery often arrives with a high school graduation announcement, such things have never bothered him.)

Shortly before leaving for the people hospital, we learned that veterinarians expect cash. But our faithful Dr. Stork has inexhaustible patience, so guess who got paid that time? There were some fringe benefits, however. Dr. Stork so enjoyed my honest recital of the Saga of Pup that he gave us a twenty-five-dollar discount. ("I can't wait to tell them about this in the doctor's lounge," he explained, wiping his eyes and choking back further fits of laughter.)

Although I know that the full fury of outraged American manhood may descend upon me, I've decided that women are far more practical than men when it's time to deal with the family budget. We're more realistic and better attuned to household math. Who but a mother would quickly calculate a simple, "Only five dollars a month!" irresistible easy-payment proposition for some luxury item, and mentally transform it into the equivalent purchase of baby food jars, pork chops, and on-sale socks? And who but a father states with manly pride, "That kid sure is shooting up, isn't he?" while ignoring the inevitable fact that Young Master Tall will soon require larger sneakers, longer jeans, and a shirt or two that reaches his newly expanded wrists?

But the real enemy of family solvency isn't the vet, the obstetrician, the butcher, or even a husband who fancies himself the reincarnation of Diamond Jim Brady. ("Say, honey, did you see this ad for a fantastic new car/trip to London/condominium in ski country?")

The ultimate danger to a balanced checkbook is the children.

Oh, they start small with their demands. This lures the holder of the family pocketbook into a false sense of security. "May I please have a penny for the bubble gum machine?" lisped by somebody who can barely turn the handle unassisted won't threaten next month's mortgage payment. But as they grow, so do their expectations.

"I need a quarter for Scout dues/library fine/a new pen because somebody snitched mine during math." Still, this period is capable of some type of maternal cash control for anybody wise enough to stock up on a little loose change. Shaking an empty change purse in front of the gang can serve as an indisputable explanation that the wolf is no longer at the door, but now hungrily prowling through the front hall. (A truly prudent woman will never explain the miracle of modern checking accounts to anyone under retirement age.)

By the time the teens roll around, however, the fat is really in the financial fire.

"Hey, Ma, can I use the charge plate? I'm going shopping for a prom dress/stereo album/tank of gas so I can use the car before our auto insurance expires."

Now we're into some truly top-level consumer demands. Her young clearly display certain signs that declare them to be the offspring of the reincarnation of Diamond Jim Brady.

"Hey, Dad, did you see this ad for a fantastic ten-speed bike/trip to Disneyland/condominium in ski country?"

After canceling the family subscription to whichever newspaper carries the most advertising, there's nothing else a mother can do except buy a tape recorder (if she can get her charge plate back from the kids). Properly programmed, it will repeat at five-minute intervals, "*Absolutely not!*" Then, allowing a few seconds for further offspring argumentation, comes the second standard recorded message: "BECAUSE WE CAN'T AFFORD IT, THAT'S WHY NOT!"

For those who have been blessed with incredibly stubborn (and/or mathematically dense) sons and daughters who are determined to pursue some additional, "But, Mom, I can't live without it!" yearnings a bit further, it might be helpful to tape a list of folks to whom the family owes the next thirteen pay checks: the pediatrician, the utility company ("You wouldn't want them to shut off our phone service, would you?" can give even the most obstinate teen-ager a moment's pause for serious reflection), the shoe store, the obstetrician (the baby is only six, so not fully paid for yet), etc. A brief reading of the local yellow pages may be in order for the woman who can't carry a complete list of creditors in her head.

Although the state of our family's budget would make a grown accountant cry, it does have certain advantages. This clan took to heart St. Paul's warning that the love of money is the root of all evil. They thoughtfully see to it that there isn't enough loot left in my purse for me to become well acquainted with, much less begin a long-term romance.

Only goodness and poverty abound in our house.

Bible Translations for the Very Married

JOAN

"Remember—Matthew 21:22!" a pen pal signed her letter yesterday.

"Matthew 21:22?" I rescued our elderly Bible from under the clothes drier and looked up the passage. "Whatever you ask for in prayer, believing, you shall receive."

"What a nice meditation," I mused. "Too bad I didn't think of it yesterday when Husband asked me if he should start breakfast, and I said yes."

Chipping away at the blackened kitchen counter tops, I continued to leaf through the pages of the Good Book. There were so many quotes, all apparently tailor-made for Husband and me. Here's a sample of what I found:

"They wandered in a wilderness, in a place without water; they found not the way of a city for their habitation. They were hungry and thirsty; their souls fainted in them" (Ps. 106:4-5).

Translation: "Can't we just stop in a gas station and ask for directions?"

29

"He sought profitable words, and wrote words most right and full of truth" (Eccl. 12:10).

Translation: "Dear Commonwealth Edison, Since my wife forgot to pay the bills last month, I'm inquiring as to the possibility of having our power turned back on . . ."

"For winter is now past, the rain is over and gone; the flowers have appeared in our land, the time of pruning is come" (Cant. 2:11–12).

Translation: "Listen, before the neighbors form a committee, can't you do *something* about the yard?"

"Better is the man that walketh in simplicity . . ." (Prov. 19:1).

Translation: "Just what do I have to do around here to get a clean pair of socks?"

"And there were flashes of lightning, rumblings and peals of thunder, and there was a great earthquake such as never has been . . . Cities fell, and every island fled away, and the mountains could not be found" (Apoc. 16: 18–20).

Translation: "Boy, that was *some* New Year's Eve party, wasn't it?"

"The wolf shall dwell with the lamb, and the leopard shall lie down with the kid; the calf and the lion and the sheep shall abide together, and a little child shall lead them" (Isa. 11:6).

Translation: "You mean you actually gave the kids permission to have their pet show in our garage?"

"Why, O Lord, are they multiplied that afflict me? Many are they that rise up against me" (Ps. 3:1).

Translation: "I guess we'll have to call off the dinner party, hon. Three of the kids are getting chicken pox."

"And he opened the bottomless pit, and there came up smoke out of the pit, and the sun and the air were darkened. And out of the smoke there came forth locusts . . ." (Apoc. 9:2–3).

Translation: "Thank heavens. I've been waiting all spring for your dad to get that basement organized."

"My bones are grown dry like fuel for the fire. My days have declined like a shadow, and my heart is withered" (Ps. 101:4, 12).

Translation: "Leave your mother alone today, guys. She's having a mid-life crisis."

"Look not round about thee in the ways of the city, nor wander up and down in the streets thereof" (Eccli. 9:7).

Translation: "I know I'm three hours late from grocery shopping, but it's the first time I've been out of the house all month!"

"In my bed by night I sought him whom my soul loveth; I sought him and found him not" (Cant. 3:1).

Translation: "What are you doing out here in the living room at this hour?"

"Just thinking."

"Thinking about what?"

"About how glad I am to be married. To you."

Blessed be the Bible.

Blessed be its holy authors.

And blessed are couples like us, who find everything we need within its pages.

The Challenge of Space

ANN

"I made a few quick calculations today," I informed Himself last night at the dinner table. "Considering the limited closet space, even more limited play space, not to mention our lone bathroom, this house was designed to hold a maximum of 3.7 people."

He drew a deep breath, cast an appraising eye over the eight offspring assembled for supper, and sadly announced, "It looks like some of you will have to go."

"Let's not be hasty," I implored, trying to lead him to the path I'd plotted. "There will be room here for everyone if we just plan carefully and open things up a bit."

With a perceptive nod, Himself set down the pie fork and reached for his ever-handy wrecking bar.

"Just tell me where you want me to start, hon," he responded enthusiastically.

Visions of past disasters flashed before my eyes. The two days he spent gleefully ripping out some badly cracked walls in the living room, happy as a preschooler handed his own box of rubber tools. The two years he took to replace the walls in the living room. (While quick to demolish, he views replacing parts of our

structure as something to be saved for dull retirement years.)
Then there was the Christmas Eve I prepared for a festive family
reunion, while he gave some last minute touch-ups to the trim
behind the couch—a project begun the previous Easter. (Wasn't
that also the time he opened the door with a paint brush clutched
between his teeth? My sister-in-law won't ever forget his greeting
kiss.)

"Maybe we should start with some rearranging, instead of leaping into a full-scale demolition project," I pleaded desperately.
"That ought to give us some idea of the proper direction to take
with future projects."

I may learn slowly, but eventually I do learn. Now I understand
exactly where we made our original mistakes. (Besides misin-
terpreting a *Double Your Money in Real Estate* book, that is,
which led us to double our family in real estate—we added four
more tots to the original four who moved into this badly cracked
domain with us.)

Yes, I've learned. Has it really been thirteen years since I informed my neighbor of our household fix-it-up philosophy?

"We've got it all worked out," I told her that dim day in history. "We're going to tackle our projects one at a time, and do
them right." (Why did she gasp for breath, I wondered? Wasn't
she feeling well? But her husband didn't seem alarmed. He sat
there, nodding with approval at our "do it right" theory.) "After
all, we don't want our place to look like Jerry's down the street.
All their bookshelves list to the left."

"He didn't use a level," deduced Mr. Neighbor.

"Should have used a level," agreed Himself. "I'm going to buy
a level before I put up those living room bookshelves Ann wants."

Eight years later he did—on the eve of Elder Daughter's grammar school graduation. While I prepared the chip dip, he
whipped out his handy-dandy circular saw and began to construct
seventy-two feet of book shelves in the middle of the freshly
polished living room. The next day our guests found themselves
collecting splinters in the most embarrassing places whenever they
perched on the couch.

"Where did we go wrong with our do-it-right theory?" I asked Mrs. Neighbor when the sawdust was nearly under control.

"You poor thing," she whispered softly as she poured me another cup of plaster-coated coffee. (Her husband had decided to remove a kitchen wall in time for her parents' fortieth anniversary party.) "They really don't want to do it right. What they'd prefer is not to do it at all. Which is why nothing gets done until they figure there's an excellent chance you'll plead with them to postpone the project—and then you might as well kiss it good-by for the next twenty years, if you do."

I toyed with the plaster chips lining my saucer.

"But Jerry . . ."

"Jerry's wife has bookshelves," Mrs. Neighbor pointed out. "Sure, they all run downhill and people can get a little seasick searching for a particular volume. But they're *there*—and they went up the day after Jerry's wife asked for them."

Mulling over this hard-won wisdom, I vowed never to turn Himself loose on another construction or destruction project. It simply wasn't worth the wear and tear on our marriage. Instead, we'd make the most efficient use of space already under our roof.

"We've got four bedrooms and need five," I estimated as I placed another slice of pie before Himself, handed him a fork, and removed the wrecking bar for secure storage under the dog's bed.

"I can cut a door into the back closet, rip out the side wall, and then"—he got a fanatic gleam in his eyes that terrified me—"if we cantilever a platform over the driveway . . ."

"There's no need to tire yourself, sweetheart," I soothed, plopping a scoop of emergency-use-only ice cream on his pie to distract him. "All we have to do is clean out the attic and move a couple of kids up there."

With that announcement, I slithered out of the dining room and dashed for the stairs, Himself in hot pursuit. The race was officially on.

"Why don't you lug this old trunk down to the garage?" I suggested in my most innocent manner. Since the garage is only one step removed from the Goodwill basket, he rebelled.

"That's got all my old army uniforms in it! We can't get rid of them!" (It's been a while since he checked his waistline. More than the size of our family has doubled in the past decade.)

"And this box of old toys too," I stated firmly.

"Uncle Herman gave me those wooden blocks. They're heirlooms—been in the family for generations!" he screamed. (They're likely to be in the family for generations more—the kids refuse to touch them.)

"Get rid of the punctured football, that pair of ice skates" (size 3, when the smallest foot that trods our family turf is a solid 10), "and this box of books can go into the kids' bookcase." (When I'm working on all cylinders, I show no mercy.)

"My Uncle Wiggily collection! I can't bear to have those little savages touch these pages," he sniffled softly. "Why don't we keep the good stuff and toss out these old rags?" he pleaded, holding up my wedding dress and veil.

Two hours and eleven tantrums later, everything in the attic was relocated to the garage, the basement, or the curbside, waiting for the morning trash pickup. It seemed safe to leave for a quick jaunt to the supermarket, providing I put Eldest Son in charge of defending the discard pile from his father's prying paws.

"Guard it with your life," I warned my firstborn.

After my return, I sliced a few carrots for the hamsters while taking mental inventory of my tribe. Sons Three and Four were happily banging drawers in the bedroom they now shared in some semblance of privacy. Stereo car-pounding drifted from the room where both daughters had retreated, since their living quarters would not be disrupted by any round-the-house relocations, and they have strong moral objections to work in any form. From the attic bedroom, I heard Son Number Two testing his big brother's drum set, although he was theoretically supposed to be putting away his underwear. The dogs circled my feet, ever hopeful some ground round would fall their way. But someone was missing.

"Where's your father?" I asked Eldest Son, who had sauntered in from his guard-the-garbage detail in search of a post-dinner snack.

"He's fine, Mom. I saw him in the garage, sitting on an old

trunk, stroking his imaginary wrecking bar and crooning, 'Uncle Wiggily, how can I get through the winter without you?' "

Something tells me it's going to be a long wait for spring. Maybe I should risk asking him to put up a couple of towel bars in the bathroom. Having his electric drill back in his hands might help him recover from his loss. Yes, it's worth taking a chance.

After all, we're not expecting any guests until July.

He Walks in Splendor

JOAN

When my spouse leaves for work in the morning, I often feel the urge to roll a red carpet from the kitchen door down to the garage. Frankly, he looks like an ad for a male modeling school—crisp shirt, perfectly tailored suit, shoes so highly glossed that one must squint if one wishes to pass them.

A casual observer might assume that Husband possesses either a full-time valet, a wealthy wife, or an uncanny sense of style and flair in order to make such a positive impression upon the waiting world. But such is not the case. Casual Observer would be aghast if he could gaze into the closet from whence this every-morning splendor emerges. How can a snappy dresser spring from such total chaos?

First of all, like many men, Husband is a pack rat. No item of wearing apparel can be discarded if there is the slightest possibility that it will one day be back in style. The jacket that he wore as a high school lifeguard (now missing both sleeves but otherwise quite serviceable) hangs next to his army parka. (Husband has worn this parka exactly twice since we were married, but one never knows when the thermometer will again dip to 35 degrees below zero.) Next to these relics hang three *other* jackets, useful, according to Spouse, for emptying trash and unclogging rain gutters (although he usually performs these jobs while wearing one of at least six paint-spattered sweatshirts cramming his dresser drawers). One must then maneuver past two raincoats (held over as sentimental tokens of the Fabulous Fifties) and a sweater upon which Eldest Son spit up for the very first time, before discovering the chic, stylish coat that Spouse is permitted to wear beyond the boundaries of our back yard.

As if the hoarding habit weren't bad enough, Husband also displays an inconsistent attitude when purchasing clothes. He will go for eight or ten months without buying an item. ("The kids need new shoes, and if I have to look at the holes in your underwear one more day, I'm going to torch your dresser.") Then, ambling casually through a department store one day, Husband will spot a sale on suspenders and go berserk, grabbing anything that is marked down 40 per cent. Which leads to some interesting moments.

"Look!" he said proudly one day. "Three pairs of plaid pants. All on sale!"

"Wonderful." I swung open his closet door, and we both stared at a rack of striped shirts. "What are you planning to wear with them?"

"Maybe I'd better pick up a few solid-color shirts," he suggested.

"Maybe some plain slacks too," I pointed out, "since the two sport coats you brought home last year are both brown checked."

"And all my shoes are black," he sighed, "except those red sneakers and my beach thongs . . ."

"Not too suitable for sales meetings," I agreed. "And I *am* fond of purple ties, but . . ." I put on my sunglasses and pointed to seven violet numbers, dangling between his navy belts.

By the time we had finished filling in Husband's wardrobe "holes," we had to postpone eating for the next few months. But he did look smart—and still does. After all, clothing possibilities are unlimited when buying for the man who has absolutely nothing.

The Impossible Athlete

ANN

Recently I noticed the following item in the newspaper: ". . . when she saw her spouse sitting in front of the TV for the fifth football game that weekend, she shot him."

Now I detest violence and could never consider such an action (even though his wounds were superficial), but I think I can understand what circumstances could trigger such a drastic reaction.

What is there about grown men and televised sports? There they sit, getting paunchier and more out of condition. Mutely they swill down beer, sandwiches, and any snack that doesn't move in the middle. The chewing stops only when they pause mid-mouthful to cheer on "their" team. "Atta wayta go, baby!" bellows around the edges of the pastrami.

Why does every adult male feel it his patriotic duty to encourage, with his constant observation, twenty-two musclebound athletes trying to pound each other through the Astro-turf?

It's easier to pry toddlers away from a candy display in the supermarket than to get fathers out of the living room during football season—which, thanks to the miracle of modern media and the almighty advertising buck, runs roughly from April to February.

Last St. Patrick's Day, my darling took a short recess to greet the children.

"My gosh, you've grown. Going into seventh grade soon, aren't you?" he fondly asked our eldest son.

"I'm a high school senior, Dad."

With all the pride of a paternal figure returning home after a decade shipwrecked on a deserted island, the Light of my Life took his place at the head of our dusty family dinner table. He smiled benevolently upon each of the children, then paled suddenly.

"There's eight of them!" he accused me. "At least you might have had the decency not to allow anyone to bring a friend home for our annual reunion dinner. Have you no sentimental family feelings at all?"

"They're all ours," I informed him. "This is the baby."

Taking the three-year-old by the hand, I led him around the table and introduced him to his father.

"When did this little guy come along?" my spouse inquired.

"During the Super Bowl, 1974. Your mother drove me to the hospital."

Obviously he didn't trust me to resist slipping in a ringer just to embarrass him.

"Wouldn't I have seen him sometime since then?" he demanded suspiciously.

"Sorry, honey. He always naps during half time. And he couldn't run the beer detail. He loves to shake the cans."

Satisfied, my partner took a critical look at the youngest, trying to etch his little image on the fatherly brain for the seasons ahead.

"Say, he walks well. When did he pick that up?" he inquired with true fatherly pride.

"Old Timers Game, 1975."

"Daddy?" the little fellow asked me, puzzled. He'd never seen his father's face before, since it had always been pasted to the set.

"Daddy," I told him, leading him to the rear. He looked at the back of his pater's pate, then repeated with satisfaction, "Daddy."

"We've missed you, dear," I assured my husband.

"I know, I know. Now, everybody, you've got to give me a quick rundown on how you're all doing with school, Scouts, and all your other activities. Anybody get married? We can't waste time. The season reruns start in twenty minutes."

I've finally figured it all out. Televised football is an extra-terrestrial plot to conquer the world. When the little green men from Mars take over, no American male will notice.

Until they get into the playoffs, that is.

Children: The Frosting on the Pizza

ANN

Some couples suffer fundamental philosophical differences over where to squeeze the toothpaste. Others disagree on proper placement of the evening paper, what TV show to watch, and open versus closed windows. For any pair so divided, there's one foolproof solution—have children.

Offspring put petty squabbles into proper perspective. A father is so pleased to *find* a toothpaste tube with any contents at all, he doesn't fret about the position of the dents. Any mother's heart leaps with joy when the television offerings are composed of something besides kiddie cartoon shows and science-fiction horrors that have been dubbed in English; she'll settle for the civilized treat of viewing Monday night football with her spouse and call herself blessed indeed. A parent is so struck with gratitude at the sight of an evening paper unblemished by crayon color charts or some space where a chain of paper dolls once filled the holes on the editorial page, he/she'll gladly read it on the roof. (Which is probably the only place the newsboy could put it without the kids reaching it first.) And the joy of opening or closing any unbroken window brings tears to parental eyes.

Children bring a heightened perception of the partner's true worth to both husband and wife. From the moment a spouse first utters, "It's us against them," a cherished alliance is formed to defend against pestilence and modeling clay in the blender.

Little ones furnish benefits beyond that of parental solidarity. The all-purpose question, "Who took my car/wrench/curling iron/razor/new socks?" can be economically answered, "The kids." People without children are forced to squander words and creative thought on such trivia. But "The mailman borrowed it" or "The dog must have buried it somewhere" lacks an element of credibility in certain cases. (When the dog is a toy poodle and the car a *Cadillac*. . . .)

The day a woman learns that Mother's Little Angel took her best girdle to Show and Tell, she needs a husbandly shoulder to cry on. If that same masculine torso shook with rage a week earlier when Daddy's Tiny Sweetheart made a bed for the cat with the tuxedo he rented for his brother's wedding, so much the better. Then his standard, soothing, "Now, honey, it could be worse," has a definite ring of truth to it. His leased ruffled shirt and magenta cumberbund no longer have their old snap either, so she'll find more sincerity in his words.

Yes, children are a blessing upon a marriage. They guarantee long years of the solid matrimonial united front necessary for parental survival. The path to genuine connubial bliss is tornadoed clear of any trivial domestic quibbles. Husbands and wives rejoice in a harmony they could not have earlier imagined. Only one phantom of discord lurks behind their present joy.

Whatever will they do when the kids leave home?

Dear Helpmate . . .

JOAN

By the time you awaken and read this note, I'll be gone. Don't panic—I haven't run away from home (although the thought is tempting—I didn't want to mention this, but I think the kids are all coming down with athlete's foot. And there may be a bee's nest in your side of the garage). No, I've just gone to tonight's Town Hall meeting without you. You looked so peaceful, snoring there on the hallway floor. How could I wake a man who's had such a hard day?

There *were* a few things I wanted to discuss with you this evening, and a note may be the perfect way. Especially since I have difficulty capsulizing my remarks into the few seconds provided by the TV commercial breaks. Yes, I realize that "Animal World" is your favorite show, but frankly I fail to see what is so exciting about watching two hippos engaged in a mating dance.

In any event, on to Item #1. As you will recall, we installed new carpeting in the family room five months ago. Have you made any decision as to when you will be replacing the doors, or moving the furniture back into the room? I realize that you disapprove of nagging wives, but it *is* getting rather difficult to cook

44

with two sofas in the kitchen. And those bookcases in the bathtub are driving me crazy! Let's pull together on this, hon, and remember our team motto. Whatever it is.

Item #2. Personally, I don't care a bit if you insist on having your entire family here for the Memorial Day weekend. I've always admired your suaveness when it comes to hosting large groups. But I am definitely vetoing your suggestion of cutting down our 100-year-old weeping willow to prevent any of our guests from falling out of it. I happen to love that tree, and if broken arms are good enough for our own offspring, they ought to be good enough for the cousins, too.

Item #3. Frankly, I think your decision to discontinue our telephone service for the entire summer seems a bit harsh. I realize that none of your business calls have gotten through since 1972, but I keep telling you we need another line. What with me being room mother again, and the kids so interested in up-to-the-minute sports and weather reports (as well as their constant attempts to get through to the White House), well, really, I'm hoping you'll reconsider.

That's about it, dear, except to remind you that if you should happen to wake up in time, you might want to meet me over at the Town Hall. Tonight's agenda involves those complaints against our garbage collectors, who keep crushing up everything they find left at the curb. The man across the street just discovered that that's what happened to his Volkswagen, and I've been wondering about our lawn mower. (I did tell you that it's missing, didn't I?)

Have a nice nap, dear.

Love and kisses,
Me

What Is a Father?

ANN

A father is someone who's learned how to watch the ball game while holding a cranky infant on his shoulder. He's a former bachelor who now has intimate knowledge of diapers, teething rings, and the cost of baby food, yet retains his dreams. In a few years, he hopes to take a course in remedial bowling just in time to enter the father-daughter or father-son tournament.

A father is somebody who can show a tiny child how to toss a ball, but never quite catches the return throw so the little one is able to laugh with Daddy at his mistakes. He's an expert in assembling new trikes, reassembling old wagons, and mending broken dolls or favorite plastic cars for a small person who trustingly says, "Please fix it, Daddy."

A father is somebody who used to remember all major league batting averages and the poker odds against drawing to an inside straight. He now channels his mathematical gifts into the field of dental bills, puppy shots, and how soon the family budget can stretch to buy three new pairs of school shoes.

A father is a guy who can explain to a tearful toddler why we don't hit the window with our hammer, tell a teen son that he has

46

to take his turn with the dinner dishes even if he does feel it's women's work, and remind a fifth-grader that this week's spelling test grade had better surpass last week's F+, or else.

A father is a man who is quite reasonable in almost every area, until he lists five sensible reasons for a fifteen-year-old's 10 P.M. curfew, then bellows, "BECAUSE I SAID SO!" after the fourth whimpering rendition of, "Why do I have to be home so early when the rest of the guys . . . ?" and feels he somehow failed in communicating with his son.

A father is a person with nerves of steel when it's time to take a teen-ager out for driving practice, yet begins pacing the floor at 9 P.M. when his trustworthy, sensible seventeen-year-old daughter isn't home from a date yet.

A father is a guy who screams, "No daughter of mine is going to volunteer for holes in her head!" when a certain offspring mentions her desire to pierce her ears. Then, he ignores the new jewelry dangling from freshly punctured lobes the following week, and secretly suggests that her mother check closely for possible infection.

A father is a person who lingers over a display of baby dolls when choosing a birthday gift for an eighteen-year-old daughter, and wonders where the years went.

What Is a Mother?

ANN

A mother is someone who used to sleep until noon who now greets each new dawn with a contented infant nodding on her shoulder. She's a woman who has discovered the wonders of disposable diapers, knitted crib sheets, and one-piece baby stretch suits, yet retains her dreams. In a few years, she hopes to take a course in remedial tennis just in time to enter the mother-son or mother-daughter tournament.

A mother is somebody who will let a tiny child watch her efficiently frost a cake, yet never quite gets the last bit of icing out of the bowl so there is something left for little fingers to lick. She's an expert in assembling budget casseroles, disassembling pies into equal portions, and mending skinned knees with a kiss and a cookie.

A mother is somebody who used to remember the names of all the latest best sellers and where to buy the nicest clothes. She now channels this retentive gift into the field of which classmate's birthday party is this Saturday and which next week, and where to buy the most sturdy jeans at the lowest prices.

A mother is a person who can explain to a tearful toddler why we don't hit our sister on the head with our toy car, tell a teen daughter that she'd better clean her room again even if she did do it only last month, and remind an eighth-grader that this time he'll cut the grass right now, or else.

A mother is a woman who is quite reasonable in almost every area, until she lists five sensible reasons for a fourteen-year-old's group-parties-only rule, then bellows, "BECAUSE I SAID SO!" after the fourth whimpering rendition of, "Why can't I single date when the rest of the girls are allowed to . . . ?" and feels she somehow failed in communicating with her daughter.

A mother is a person with nerves of steel when it's necessary to examine a freely bleeding head wound, yet falls apart the first time her trustworthy, sensible sixteen-year-old son takes the car to the store for a loaf of bread.

A mother is the gal who screams, "No son of mine is going to behave like a savage!" when a certain offspring mentions his desire to join the football team. Then, she spends the next three months washing team jerseys, athletic pants, sweat socks, and prays a lot at the sidelines during every game.

A mother is the person who lingers over a display of wooden trains when choosing a birthday gift for an eighteen-year-old son and wonders where the years went.

Just a Normal,
Average Woman . . .

Home Is Where the Housework Waits

ANN

The urge to organize my household, establish a workable routine, formulate the appropriate daily schedule, clean ALL the drawers and closets—not to mention the attic, basement, and garage— well, it's on me again.

Perhaps I should lie down until this feeling passes. Why this periodic compulsion to battle against my basic nature and our long-standing pattern of "casual" living? I've always felt a strong bond with my favorite aunt—the one my mother described perfectly as "a good old slob."

My sporadic craving to improve efficiency and general sanitation standards may be due to some latent tendency toward martyrdom. Why else this sudden urge to enter (much less excavate) the teen-agers' rooms? It can also be triggered by specific phenomena. A new copy of any gorgeous home magazine—especially when it features an article, "Your Home Makes a Statement"— will do it. The first hint of true spring or fall weather sets it off. So does a chat with any one of my well-organized friends. (The adage that "opposites attract" must be true. Otherwise, why would I have so many neat-and-tidy chums?)

There's Joan, who zips through her housework every morning, one hand dangling daintily behind her back. By 9:05 she's done six loads of laundry, planned menus for the next four months, ordered new curtains and a spread for the master bedroom, and regrouted her upstairs bathroom tile.

And Dorie, who has a gift for stripping all the beds in her house, swishing them through the washer, and drier and having them back on the mattresses (ironed, of course) in less than ten minutes. I often suspect lint doesn't dare gather under her furniture, due to the whirlwind pace at which she moves.

Or my fantastic sister-in-law, who singlehandedly keeps a ten-room house immaculate, tends five acres of lush shrubbery, volunteers three mornings a week at the local grammar school, and participates in six car pools. She also excels in gourmet cooking and regularly throws intimate little dinner parties for thirty. There must be some secret to her ability hidden under that exquisite mop of naturally curly hair.

Perhaps I should stop surveying my friends' well-ordered domiciles and try to find some bonus points in my own. If every cloud has a silver lining, there has to be some fringe benefit lurking under the cluttered life style around here.

Neighbors always feel free to drop by without formal invitation. They know it won't upset my "routine," and my coffeepot is always eager to perk a few cups for the discouraged soul seeking comfort in another sink filled with not-yet-done dishes.

If I were more efficient, would my husband have been content to work at his own pace when we redecorated the living room? Granted his own pace took two years (snails passed by and let out a scornful "Slowpoke!" during the project), and we wore out two sets of slipcovers before the painting was finished. But it looks great anyway. If I were really well ordered, could I have happily coexisted with a man whose painting schedule calls for repairing one crack every third weekend? And whose building tendencies burst forth in the construction of a lovely set of bunk beds (in the middle of the still-unpainted living room) the night before Eldest Son's graduation party?

Would my children feel as free to bring home friends, stray animals, and huge pieces of dead tree limb if they had another kind of mother? Oh, they know I'll yell and scream when I see the results of their latest trip through the neighborhood trash piles. But once the howling subsides, they can get on with their creative efforts. We've got a clay model reconstruction of the planet Saturn (complete with rings) on the front porch, an in-progress clubhouse emerging from the scrap lumber pile in the basement, and goodness-knows-what growing under the beds.

What other home on the block would automatically open its door to lost or injured animals? Who else would tolerate a limping hawk cloistered in a borrowed bird cage? Or answer a husband's homecoming "What's new, honey?" with the announcement that there's a beagle in the basement?

At this very moment, there are six small boys (only some of whom live here) fashioning finger-paint murals on the kitchen floor (some of it on paper), two high school daughters (both of whom live here) constructing tennis dresses and a monumental mess in the dining room, and a pair of teen-age sons working in the vegetable garden. (They chose that labor as an alternative to cleaning their room.)

Interior decorators often proclaim that houses should reflect the people who live in them, and I bow to that theory. Ours definitely reflects us. There's only one thing that still bothers me.

What kind of statement is being made by the hamster condominium that holds the most prominent place in the middle of our newly painted living room?

Mirror, Mirror on the Wall ...

JOAN

Several months ago, my husband eyed me strolling through the house in my nine-year-old blue bathrobe and suggested that perhaps some charity ought to throw a tag day for me.

"This robe is perfectly good!" I protested.

"Good for what?" he wanted to know.

Actually, he's right. My wardrobe is so pathetic that even our gerbils refuse to nest in my closet. Two good outfits—a pants suit and a long dress—hang majestically swathed in plastic, and the rest is a hodge-podge of baggy jeans, pilling sweaters, and a collection of spike-heeled pumps. My talented mother occasionally makes me an outfit (she well remembers the day I was expelled from high school sewing class for flunking Needle Threading), but other than these contributions, I'm a mess.

But where does a woman begin? "Start with Separates," advises the fashion section of my newspaper. Fine. Except that the separates blazer I'm going to start with costs forty-nine dollars, leaving me with just enough small change for the bus trip home, and nothing new to match it. I could buy a separate blouse and a separate skirt instead. Except that the blouse—a sleeveless print number—looks a bit odd with the wool plaid skirt I've selected.

Fashion-conscious women often use new accessories to spruce up a well-worn ensemble, I've heard. But this must be a special art, because tying a new scarf around the neck of my 1963 middy blouse doesn't seem to do a thing for it—or me.

Then there's the question of budgeting. Does it make more sense to buy a few designer items and wear them forever, or to settle for lots of chintzy things that can be tossed at the first sign of a ripped seam? One of my friends, who admits her designer is Monsieur Clarence Racque, opts for the second plan, undergoing a complete wardrobe turnover every few months. (She gets to wear each item twice before her daughters confiscate it.) Another acquaintance purchases only clothing in the three-digit price-tag range. But since her husband has declared bankruptcy four times in the last two years, I'm not sure this is the way to go.

One solution is to find a store with nifty merchandise, open a charge account, and go on a buying binge every six months or so—depending heavily on the saleswoman's advice and mercy. Unfortunately, when faced with a sleek, perfectly groomed saleswoman, I turn into a mass of inferior jelly, and can barely open my mouth, much less fall to my knees weeping and pleading.

If clothes aren't difficult enough, there's also the matter of hair care and make-up. Talk about intimidating experiences! I still remember the day, while dripping over the shampoo bowl, I overheard the salon manager talking to his assistant:

"Do you think we can save her?"

"With the grace of God. But it'll be a long, uphill climb, sir."

"Well, let's try and win this one for the Gipper."

It's nice to be noticed, but I still wish they hadn't brought in all the students from the beauty academy next door. Imagine how it feels to be presented as the perfect example of "Before."

"You'll go a long way before you see someone as neglected as this, class," the salon manager announced over his bullhorn. The students stared at me and nodded solemnly.

Actually, my problem is a common one. As I trip into the

swivel chair, my beautician lifts a strand of wet hair and says, "How do you want it done?"

Resisting the impulse to scream, "For Pete's sake, how should I know? That's why I'm HERE!" I smile sweetly and ask, "What do you suggest?"

She shrugs.

"Why don't I shave it, and then you can amble through our wig department."

Assuming my finished hair style doesn't leave the shop personnel paralyzed with laughter, I usually move on to the cosmetic counter. Perhaps here I will discover just the product to transform me from Ms. Dowdy into a suburban siren.

"What can I do for you?" asks the salesgirl, whose white and purple lip gloss reflects her dazzling green eye shadow.

I sigh.

"Got anything in pink?"

"You'd better do something with those nails." She peers at my fingers.

"I just had a manicure."

"Oh."

There is one solution to my quest for beauty and fashion expertise. My husband will have to become President of the United States. Then designers and make-up artists will beat a path to my door (and be sworn to official secrecy about my frayed bra straps and graying roots). Until the Inauguration, however, I guess I'm stuck with my old blue robe, pancake make-up, and split ends.

Being beautiful isn't everything, people say. But wouldn't it be fun to find out?

This Is Progress?

ANN

For some time, I considered the electric-powered trash compactor to be the height of gadget-giddiness in an overtechnologized society.

How wrong I was!

That was before the introduction of the non-electric trash compactor—the one where the house-person inserts the trash, then sits on the lid to do the mashing. My old age (or my parenthood of six sons) may be showing, but this seems just a device to replace the boy who, when told the garbage is overflowing (in futile hopes he will remove it), puts one of his size sixes, sevens, or eights solidly on top of the cascading debris, stomps firmly once or twice, and proudly announces, "You've got lots of room in there now, Mom."

He has developed the avoidance of carry-out labor to a fine art. Now modern manufacturers have enabled people without children of trash-toting age to know the same joy. As my husband astutely pointed out while watching a half-time commercial for a trash compactor, "It's just great in theory—only one trip a week out with the garbage. But I'd develop a hernia or slipped disc, lugging the nicely compacted accumulation from this clan out to the curb."

Modern science has also bestowed on us those marvelous polyethylene bags which, with exquisite timing, split under the weight of their contents just before reaching the outdoor garbage receptacles. It is debatable whether they are an actual improvement on the free brown paper grocery bags, designed to self-destruct at the drop of a tea bag, right there in the kitchen. Non-compacting people have their troubles too.

Automatic ice-crushers now take the place of young fellows with hammers, who once pounded newspaper-wrapped ice cubes on the basement floor as their contribution to a family party. I suspect it's all part of some ZPG plot to increase parties and decrease kids.

Every young man used to serve a carving apprenticeship under his father, as he mastered this art once proper to the Head of the House. The little gadget used to sharpen the implements has been made obsolete by a slot on the electric can opener. And the ritualistically honed tools have given way to the electric knife, making it possible for a kindergarten student to dispatch the surgical job.

Our plug-in knife has been on the premises less than a year, but how far we've fallen into the pit of technological decadence. Gone are the days when the children would "oooh" and "ahhh" as perfect slices of turkey or ham fell before Daddy's artistically employed blade.

Last week the three year-old appropriated my table knife and pretended to cut his spaghetti. While waving the utensil, he made strange noises.

"What's wrong with him?" demanded his concerned father.

No one had any theories until the four-year-old volunteered:

"He's using an electric knife."

Since then, this little child of the almost twenty-first century has gone engineering science one better. He now pretends he's eating with an electric fork.

Perhaps I should accept all these "progressive" developments with good grace. But I can't stand the thought of a future generation hearing my children refer to the use of all these AC-DC gizmos as part of the "good old days."

Ode to Old Betsy

JOAN

To be a suburban matron, only two things are necessary: one must own a tract house on a street named Happy Hollow, Boll Weevil Drive, or a reasonable facsimile thereof. And one must run at least eight car pools per week.

During our first six years in suburbia, I was excluded from true membership in the boondocks sorority for the simple reason that ours was a one-car family—and my husband was usually in it. Nose pressed against the window, I would watch as my liberated neighbors chugged to and fro, gliding from one exotic locale to another—while I worried about who would bring in the daily milk supply, or oiled up my bicycle for another mad fling around the block.

"You *have* to get a car," a supportive friend brainwashed me. "Tell you what—I'll sell you mine. It just needs a few minor repairs."

"Thanks," I told her, "but don't you think a missing steering wheel and only three tires is more than *minor*?"

But she was right.

"I have to get a car," I told my husband. "Everyone else ends

61

up chauffeuring our kids around. I'm starting to feel like a leech."

"As soon as we can afford it," Husband soothed.

"I'll be in the Holy Angels rest home by that time," I snapped. "We can afford all kinds of other luxuries now—like pot roasts and dentists. Why can't I have a car?"

Whether fate intervened, or St. Christopher took a personal interest in my traveling problems, I will never know. But one summer day, Spouse fell in love with a snappy new model (a *car*), and brought our old rig in for a trade-in estimate.

"You're not going to believe this," he told me indignantly. "The dealer said $200 was his top price."

"He's only giving us $200?"

"No—we have to pay *him* to haul Old Betsy away."

Our eyes met. I was a car owner at last.

Old Betsy and I suited each other like ice cream and chocolate sauce. We were both rusted in the same places, and had similar problems waking up in the morning. A hopelessly out-dated duo, we also shared a chronic cough and knew full well that no amount of cosmetic cover-ups could camouflage our basic defects. It was a perfect union.

Perfect, that is, until the kids intervened. Children who previously could hike to a neighboring state suddenly developed paralysis when faced with an extra car in the driveway.

"Mom, can you drive me to Joey's house?"

"Joey lives next door."

"I know, but it's 40 degrees out there!"

"Ready to go, Mom? My bowling team kicks off in five minutes."

"Hey, no fair! She's supposed to drive me to work!"

"Why don't you kids ever ride your bikes any more?"

They stared as if I had just begun speaking in tongues.

Even more unsettling was my inability to comprehend mechanical details. Before car ownership, I had been concerned with only two facets of driving—the location of my keys, and the amount of gas in said vehicle. As a bona fide title-holder, however, I discovered that Husband expected me to take full responsibility for Betsy's well-being. Aside from investigating the occasional clunketys and pings under her hood (if I could get it open), that also meant boning up on oil changes (how often?), air pressure (how much?) and carburetors (why?). It was tricky, but within a few months I had discovered the secret to good car maintenance: Find a decent mechanic, write him into your will, always stay in the right-hand lane, and pray a lot.

My first year as an auto owner also provided many learning experiences. I discovered that a gas gauge resting on "E" actually *means* "E." I learned that one does not attempt to slam on one's brakes while doing fifty in a hailstorm. And on one memorable occasion, I also found out that smoking in traffic court is forbidden, even if your case has not yet been called.

All in all, it was a stimulating year, and Husband and I recently shared a toast on Betsy's hood in honor of our successful venture.

"Being a two-car family isn't all that bad," mused Spouse (who hasn't driven a kid anywhere since last fall), "even though my calculations show that Betsy is costing you $1.67 per mile."

"It was money well spent." I patted her dented fender wistfully and tried to choke back my tears. "I'm going to miss this old beauty."

"Miss Betsy? Are you getting rid of her?"

"You could say that." I blew my nose. "But it's not *my* idea."

"I don't understand," Spouse started, but he was interrupted by our two high-schoolers galloping around the corner of the driveway.

"Guess what came in the mail?" Eldest shouted. "We both passed our driving tests! Mom, can I take the car to work?"

"Hey, no fair," yelled Younger. "My bowling team kicks off in five minutes!"

I looked at Husband and he looked at me.

"It was a wonderful year, Betsy," we sighed. "So long."

Some Suggestions for
a More Liberal Education

ANN

•

It may be called domestic science these days, or perhaps bachelor living. But home economics by any other name still covers the fundamentals—cooking, cleaning, laundry, and how to choose the necessary goodies involved in these tasks. I weep whenever I recall that fatal day when I opted for an "important" subject like Philosophies of the Orient instead of good old reliable home ec.

It's time, however, to update this critical corner of the practical curriculum. Let's stop wasting energy seeking new titles for the course and instead concentrate our efforts on expanding specific areas to prepare boys and girls better for the challenge of future life.

The lab surroundings definitely call for some modernization. What student is ready to shift his/her labors from the color-coordinated, latest gadget-equipped Home Ec room to the reality of that first apartment? (The one with the microscopic refrigerator, a stove that works only when whacked in the proper place, and plumbing fixtures that talk back.) How many emerging experts know that having the right change is much more important to

64

laundromat success than using the right detergent? (Not everyone will be offered fifty dollars for an old shirt that some TV ad will transform into two rags in order to compare the action of various types of bleach.)

Once kids are aware that all is not perfect in the real-life equipment line, their school experience needs a bit more realism in a few other areas. Take the subject of laundry, for instance. (Better yet, take the laundry—PLEASE!) Properly educated, self-sufficient young people know how to choose the right equipment (but not how to pay for it), then select the appropriate combinations of detergent, bleach, and all the other possible non-phosphate additives. (The environment should be as clean as the underwear when the wash is finished.) They're well versed on fabrics, water temperatures, and how to remove stains. (Clever scholars check the chart on the back of the detergent box.) A few astute adolescents even know how to read the easy-care tags inside the clothes.

But our students still have many miles to travel before they're able to deal with real-life laundry. Washing clothes is only the surface task. Although each might be prepared to set up a business operation geared to handle all the soiled haberdashery produced by the population of Minneapolis, not one is ready for the challenges of a normal family's washday. More than suds control is involved here. They need to be introduced to the diagnostic symptoms of real, live kids. Home ec still doesn't cover the telltale topic of laundry voids, and what each one signifies.

None of his underwear slipping down the chute for several days means that the third-grader stashed his comic book collection in the bathroom again. He hasn't been in the tub for a week, except to read. (Before he artfully dampens the soap, sprinkles the bath mat, and swears he did remember to scrub behind his ears this time, that is.)

No socks in the to-be-sudsed pile is a tip-off that all those offspring who just announced, "My room's clean now, Mom," have a treasure-trove of dirty footwear stashed somewhere under the beds, and should be sent back immediately to excavate further. (This trick is what gains mothers their reputation for having eyes that can see around corners, up the stairs, and right through dust ruffles.)

There will be times, students should learn, when much can also be deduced from extra garments in the pile.

Five blouses means a high school daughter had trouble deciding which outfit to wear yesterday. (Best remedy for this condition is to assign her an hour at the ironing board, since she probably hasn't bothered to read the "tumble dry and remove immediately" tags inside those togs, so hasn't learned ironing belongs to an obsolete era.)

Three football jerseys indicate two team members will be wondering where they left their uniforms after last week's game, but not until they start suiting up for next week's gridiron battle. (Proper handling here means to launder the trio, then send halfback son to clothe the naked pair trying to explain a unique burglary to their coach before the kickoff whistle.)

But family life is not bounded by laundry alone. Among the other indispensible items that should be added to an ideal expanded lesson plan are:

1) how to remove spots on a nine-foot ceiling caused when a Cub Scout dabbled with physics and shook his pop bottle "just to see what would happen to the bubbles";

2) three easy ways to get peanut butter out of a dog's ear;

3) some foolproof method of barbecuing chicken for twenty on a twelve-inch grill;

4) what to do when "nobody" stuffs a toothbrush, three pipe cleaners, and a box of toothpicks down the drain that empties the bathroom sink (but only in theory, judging by the high tide therein);

5) how to construct a before-payday meal using the ingredients on hand: half a box of macaroni, three slightly dehydrated hot dogs, five limp carrot sticks, and a package of frozen cauliflower. (This must be transformed into a gourmet delight for a family of ten, eight of whom heartily detest vegetables in any form.)

My dream course would also require a most practical final exam. I'd gladly surrender my kitchen/laundry room/cleaning supplies to any student determined to meet a real challenge. The scholar able to toss together a seven-course feast, reorganize storage areas, match up all stray socks into tidy pairs, take twenty-three telephone messages for absent teens, and simultaneously deliver seven puppies under the kitchen table while entertaining a Cub Scout den, automatically qualifies for an A+.

To the hardy soul who survives this final exam, there are compensations far beyond grade point average. Any student, male or female, who triumphs over such a normal day in the life of a household has earned the confidence that he/she is fully prepared to face the future.

After all, bachelor living doesn't last forever.

Count-Down to Party-Time

JOAN

You have your invitation, you've decided what to wear, and the baby-sitter has been notified. Now there's nothing much to do until it's time to leave for the party, right?

Except:

Put baby in playpen, turn on Saturday morning cartoons for kids, take out ironing board. Press long skirt for you and white shirt for Husband. Be careful of jelly on four-year-old's hands. Sponge off skirt. Press again.

Start on gelatin mold for party. Send ten-year-old to store for walnuts. Change baby. Hold ladder for Husband, who is plastering bathroom ceiling. Take party clothes upstairs to avoid plaster dust. Rescue baby from bathtub. Caution Husband about swearing in front of children.

Send ten-year-old back to store with note explaining difference between peanuts and walnuts. Put baby down for early nap so she will sleep easily for sitter. Take four-year-old out of bathtub. Caution Husband again.

Make lunches. Remind eight-year-old it is not his turn to entertain neighborhood children. Make more sandwiches for neighbor children.

Husband out of plaster. Take four-year-old along to store for plaster. Stop to buy walnuts.

Gelatin mold is too hard. Begin again. Baby needs changing. Put rollers in hair and pluck eyebrows while four-year-old watches. Be careful of rollers sitting on back of toilet.

Scold four-year-old. Ask Husband to bring plunger. Caution Husband about language.

Plumber can come on short notice. Make large pot of strong coffee for plumber who says yours is best in neighborhood. Ask ten-year-old to push baby in stroller in front of house. Shave legs. Ask eight-year-old to push baby in stroller in front of house. Break up fight. Push baby in stroller.

Add walnuts to gelatin mold. Plumber is gone. Caution Husband. Pack evening bag, lay out gloves. Polish shoes while four-year old watches. Hide shoe polish.

Launder bedspread and four-year-old. Hide shoe polish again. Start dinner. Manicure nails. Husband is napping; has had hard day. Change baby. Feed, bathe, and pajama baby. Do not spindle or mutilate. Put in playpen. Call family to table. Wipe up spilled milk. Husband is in charge. Caution Husband.

Shower, put on underwear and bathrobe. Put four-year-old in pajamas. Clear table. Remind Husband to take shower before dishwasher goes on. List doctor and party phone numbers for sitter. Clean up living room for sitter. Apply make-up. Review rules and regulations with older children. Break up fight. Review rules again.

Put baby in bed. Ignore tantrum. Put on nylons and shoes. Remind Husband that plaster dust *can* get in upstairs closet. Help Husband brush navy blue suit. Rescue four-year-old from puddle in driveway. Re-pajama four-year-old. Ask Husband to spank four-year-old. Do not caution Husband about language.

Take down hair. Comb. Try again. Put on blouse and long skirt. Avoid four-year-old. Welcome sitter. Remind sitter of rules and regulations.

Leave for party. Husband is not speaking. Return to house. Pick up gelatin mold. Re-pajama four-year-old. Remind sitter of puddle in driveway. Comb hair again. Start dishwasher. Put diapers in washing machine. Wash hands. Comb hair again.

Get back in car. Do not speak to Husband. Do not pass Go. Do not collect $200.

What Hath Noah Wrought?

ANN

"It was just like walking into a zoo," Himself commented when he returned from a family errand. Neatly side-stepping a race between the dog and her half-grown puppy, he continued:

"A dog and a cat greeted me at the door." He made his usual artful dodge as the bird swooped playfully toward his head, its two-foot wing span shadowing his face.

"I don't know," he mused, shaking some fish food into one of the aquariums. "Some people are a little strange. Just as I went into their living room, one of those clear plastic exercise balls rolled across the rug with a gerbil in it."

He nimbly avoided the clear plastic ball containing a white rat which careened across our rug.

"They must have three tanks of tropical fish," he reported as four bunnies scampered by. "Why do people want to spend so much time looking after pets?" he pondered slowly while the tortoise strolled into the dining room.

"I'd never tolerate such foolishness," he assured me, ignoring the puppy that jumped into his lap. "Remember the time I told the kids firmly that they could not, ABSOLUTELY could not, have a snake?"

"Yes, dear," I soothed him. "And you were just as firm with their requests for a skunk as a substitute. By the way, you never told me where you found the tadpoles you brought home as a consolation gift."

"Fellow at work got them out of his lily pond," he grinned, stroking the kitten curled across his shoulder.

"We do have to be firm," I reminded him. "Otherwise there's no telling what these kids might bring home. You did speak to Mary about the hamster she smuggled in last Sunday, didn't you?"

"I said I would, didn't I?" he grumbled.

"How did she take it?" I worried. "She's so sensitive."

"I handled it beautifully," he admitted humbly. "I pointed out that we had all the pets we could conveniently handle. There's the sparrow hawk Joe brought home, Tom's white rat, Bob's bunnies, Ann's tank of fish, Steve's puppy, Christopher's kitten, and Billy's tadpoles. Quite enough for any family—especially when we add in the jointly owned dog and turtle."

"You make an effective case," I admired. "But are you sure she wasn't upset?"

"Of course she wasn't upset. She simply saw the logic of my position."

Suddenly he shifted his position on the couch, and a strange squeak emerged from one pocket.

"You fraud!" I accused the guilty party. "You didn't take back that hamster after all!"

"I most certainly did," declared the Ruler of the Roost. "I took it back just like I promised."

"Empty those pockets!" I ordered my Lord and Master. Shamefacedly, he reached into the roomy pockets of his favorite around-the-zoo pants, and out came . . .

"TWO hamsters!" I began to sob. "Why in the world did you bring home two hamsters? You were supposed to return the one Mary got, not come up with a spare."

"Honey, what else could I do?" he pleaded. "She pointed out

that everyone else has his or her own pets. And you did say that it was a bit lonely for the poor hamster, all alone in that cage . . ."

"I intended to have it rejoin its family somewhere else, not invite the rest of its relatives to move in here."

"Don't lose your grip, honey," he crooned, patting my trembling shoulder. "After all, what's one pet, more or less?"

Quiz for a Supermarket Freak

JOAN

1. If peas are priced at two cans for sixty-nine cents and frozen broccoli boxes weigh ninety kilograms each, shouldn't I buy carrots instead?

2. If Child A sits in the basket seat, undoing the chocolate chips, Child B lies across the lower deck complaining that he may throw up, and Child C has discovered that potato chips are on sale, why am I here?

3. If I am wearing bobby socks, a blouse torn under one arm, and a very shiny nose, will I meet Jackie-O or Liz at the frozen chicken section?

4. If pork prices have stabilized, the winter wheat crop was bumper, and citrus fruits are in season, why will I be nine dollars short in the check-out line?

5. If I have a seven-cents off coupon on Cereal X, a newspaper ad for a two-for-one margarine sale, and seventy-four trading stamps for my premium book, shouldn't we become vegetarians?

6. If an end-aisle display of beach balls is erected at 9:05 A.M., how fast can I get the kids out of the store?

7. After the contents of sixteen paper bags have been unloaded and put away, who will be the first to ask, "When are you going shopping, Mom?"

Notes I Wish I'd Never Read

ANN

In a household like ours, good communications are a must. How else can we co-ordinate the activities of ten people? But the traffic in and out sometimes makes face-to-face chats impossible.

To deal with this problem, we've finally employed written messages posted prominently where everyone is sure to see them—right on the refrigerator door. Even Himself, who swears he does no between-meal snacking, but only takes inventory from time to time (and last week inventoried his way through two chicken legs, a meat-loaf sandwich, and the last piece of pie), has developed the habit of checking our Communications Center, where everything is neatly magnetized onto the door. It's possible now to achieve afterschool sustenance and catch up with the family news during the same kitchen stop.

Frequently I find myself quivering when I read the notes posted there with shiny red apple or inviting yellow banana magnets. Our communications outlet has filled me in on more than I really wanted to know about some of this tribe's activities. Perhaps it wouldn't be so bad if I confined my reading to things meant for me. But being the kind of person who'll study the nutritional re-

75

quirements on a cereal box whenever there's nothing else to peruse, I can't resist glancing over notes meant for other folks too. Among the items I wish I'd missed were:

"Dad. Please wake me before you leave for work. I want to explain about the car." (Since the truthful soul who preferred to confess in person forgot to sign his/her name, I combined perking the morning coffee with a struggle to remember which teen had used the car last night. Himself, never one for such subtleties in a time of crisis, galloped through the house in a wake-up frenzy, pulling everyone beyond playpen age out of the sack.)

"Sis. Some guy called and said he'll meet you at the Pizza Parlor Saturday night." (This is going to cause a lot of yelling and screaming, as soon as Sis discovers Little Brother didn't bother to get the caller's name. Is it Dreamboat or Deadly Dull?)

"Jerk. Keep your hands off my stuff." (Although there was no signee or addressee, this resulted in a few days when everyone kept his hands off everyone else's stuff but mine. They know I'm fonder of screaming than scribbling during my search for the tape/scissors/pantyhose I thought had been safely hidden away.)

"Anybody. Can I borrow three dollars until payday? I'm desperate." (This poor soul is broke but honest. Of course, when the handwriting belongs to Himself, I reel under visions of cooking by candlelight, if he didn't pay the electric bill before running out of loot.)

"Dad. The doctor called. He said to give Mom a stiff drink before you tell her the rabbit died." (Who's going to give Dad a stiff drink?)

Sometimes the messages in our communications corner are meant for me. This makes me even more nervous than eavesdropping on somebody else's, since I'm usually expected to do something about them.

"Mom. When you're at the store today, will you please get a couple of things for me? I need lip gloss—be sure it's Tempting Raspberry this time—face soap, and a gallon of that super shampoo to take back to school. As long as you're out anyway, will you please pick up my winter wardrobe at the cleaner's?" (College

Daughter couldn't resist blowing last week's pay check at the Cozy Corner Boutique, and is broke again.)

"Honey. I forgot to mention I'm going to Toledo for three days." (Maybe he forgot to tell me about the Toledo trip, but I'm sure he remembered my mother's coming for a short visit.)

"Mom. I'm going to be a deer in the class play tomorrow. I can wear brown pants and shirt, so all you have to make is the antlers." (There should be a law against discovering something like this after a lively school board meeting that kept me out until midnight—especially when it's written by a fourth-grade kid who doesn't own a brown shirt and pants.)

"Honey. Don't forget to pick up something nice for the boss's daughter's wedding gift. Spend as much as necessary, as long as you keep it under $7.98." (He hasn't been in the department stores for years. Maybe I should send him to gather up College Daughter's Tempting Raspberry and other assorted supplies as part of his over-all consumer education.)

Still, there have been a few times when the Communications Center worked to my advantage. Otherwise where would I have posted my latest message to Himself?

"Darling. I'm at the store buying your favorite wine and some nice thick steaks for dinner. By the way, the body and fender shop called, and the car is going to look the way it used to when they finish with it."

Last week I found a message that made my skin crawl:

"Don't open the basement door until I get home and have a chance to explain." (Since this missive comes from our wildlife-loving offspring, it's impossible to guess what's in the basement that needs explaining. Snakes? The entire inventory of experimental animals he kidnaped from the school's science lab? A kitten from the desperate gal across the street, to whom I solemnly vowed that, if she didn't give my kids one from her cat's latest litter, I wouldn't let her kids take a puppy from ours?)

Frequently I'm tempted to take my colorful magnets and turn them into some kind of plastic fruit salad. Lack of communication can be a blessing. But as I reach for my paring knife, I notice something scrawled on a half-sheet of paper towel with bright red crayon that makes it all worth while. Past quivers and quakes fade into nothingness, when I read a message to lift my heart and brighten my day:

"I love you."

Tomorrow I'll buy some carrot, broccoli, and cauliflower magnets. There's lots of space on the side of that refrigerator we haven't used yet.

Where the Elite Meet

JOAN

It is an inescapable fact of life that as long as there are people in this world, there will be committees. And as a sort of penalty for lying around eating bonbons all day, housewives who don't "work" will be expected to join them.

Frankly, my civic pride compels me to labor at some outside task for the betterment of society. But despite the lure of the League of Women Wranglers or the Clean Sewers Committee, I find myself resisting their advances. I much prefer being a member of the lunchroom squad.

It's an elite group, of course. Only mothers who are partially deaf, sport thirty-nine-inch biceps, and own a matched set of chest protector and shin guards are eligible for membership. But these are the basic qualifications. A potential squad-person must also document an allergy to sedatives, since her job demands nerves of fine-tuned steel, and an ability to move as if she had just been shout out of a cannon.

The lucky woman who finds herself pledged to the lunchroom sorority will undergo basic training with a more experienced member of the team.

"Notice," my instructor shouted as the students streamed

through the doors, "that children are not allowed to leave the lunchroom while carrying a fork or a slice of watermelon. No one may go out to the playground unless he or she is wearing clothes. Shoving a banana up a neighbor's ear is strictly forbidden."

Just then a sixth-grade boy, bearing a striking resemblance to Attila the Hun, exploded a full milk carton with his teeth. Without breaking stride, my instructor tossed him onto the light fixture, and continued:

"If it's hamburger day, the children are not permitted to bring ketchup dispensers to the table. No karate lessons in the bathrooms. And when you see the kids stampeding to the door, you will know that the playground bell has rung. We mothers never seem to hear it."

She studied me closely.

"You look awfully puny. Are you sure your health insurance policy is in force?"

I nodded.

With heads held high, the proud sisterhood who survived lunchroom duty then marched to the playground. Collecting steel helmets and clubs, we circulated among the ranks, dodging games of maul-ball and the fourth-grade Kamikazi troop.

"No bicycle riding allowed!" shrieked my instructor as she plucked a twelve-year-old off his Honda and sent him sailing through a third-story window. The bike wobbled into a snowbank where it was immediately dismantled by the kindergarten mechanics class. I dodged a flying bowling ball and reminded myself to draw up my will at the first opportunity.

Actually, the only casualty on my initiation day was a tall young man who was carried off the field by the school paramedics.

"Too bad," my instructor shouted at me through cupped hands. "He was the nicest principal we've ever had."

I have sung in choral groups, punched doorbells during elections, and served on numerous club boards. But never have I felt so totally fulfilled as the day I was officially sworn into membership on the lunchroom squad. For only one who daily walks through the Valley of the Shadows can appreciate how wonderful it is to be alive.

Sewing Boxes and Tool Kits

ANN

Here I sit, Father, with my mountain of mending around me. There are buttons to replace on baby creepers and teen-agers' blouses. New patches to put on the knees of old jeans, for boys who spend much of their time observing the wonders of Your universe closely—the ants parading down a crack in the sidewalk, tiny shoots growing in the garden, the interesting things that can only be studied by fellows who get down on their hands and knees for a good, long look. Cuffs on school pants to be let down, bought and taken up not long ago for a junior high student who grew so rapidly.

My husband has his own repair work to do, Lord. The tool bench is covered with small cars needing replacement wheels, a locomotive that won't run, and the radio whose plug requires a bit of jiggling before it will play. There's something loose in the girls' hair drier, and the five-year-old can't ride his bike properly until the seat is raised again.

We parents spend so much time fixing things, Father. I must stitch the tail back on the baby's balding plush tiger before bedtime so he'll have his faithful companion with him when he falls asleep. The kindergartner will rest contentedly too, for he has

81

Daddy's promise that his bike will be ridable tomorrow. So the two of us have taken up our hammers, screwdrivers, needles and pins in order to keep faith with those who trust us to fix anything.

Some things can wait a bit, Lord, and probably will. That's why we always have these stacks of "I'll get around to it when I have the chance" things in the basket and on the bench. Perhaps we should try harder to keep up with our task, but there always seems to be something more important to do.

There are those other repair jobs, Father, which can't fit into the basket or on the bench, the ones requiring immediate attention. These are the mending chores we must do on the children themselves. And somehow they take precedence over those we do with our household tools.

Someone who falls from his still-a-bit-too-big-for-him bike has to be mended right away. Oh, a bandage will take care of his skinned knee. But he also needs a hug, a light dusting, and a large transfusion of confidence. Then he's able to tackle the challenge once more, with a parent watching (and praying) to see if he'll get the hang of it this time. A few quick repairs to his spirit have set him free to try again.

Sometimes all we can do is understand a disaster from the child's point of view. Then we share his misery without reminding him that life goes on. This is a discovery he must make for himself, a discovery that becomes easier when he knows he has his parents' sympathy.

The preteen who didn't make the baseball team needs a long, quiet, companionable walk with his father much more than he needs a pep talk. Spending that time with Dad, who understands, who suffers with him, who doesn't give him a rousing "let's keep this thing in perspective" lecture can work miracles. When he senses his father's pride in him, unconnected to any athletic abilities, he can gather courage to find his own perspective. Then back he goes to the ball field, this time wholeheartedly to cheer his pals through the season.

A daughter left uninvited at prom time needs some special handling, too. Perhaps her mending starts when she learns her mother once went through the same disaster. Then when her father grabs her for an impromptu waltz around the living room, she knows she's still his princess and always will be.

New shoelaces may make the fourth-grader's trip to school a little easier. But knowing that his parents understand, and are silently cheering for him to master those difficult times tables, lifts his heart to match his properly shod feet. A boy who's loved, even if he's not a mathematical genius, is a boy who can resolve to get the better of the stubborn figures if it takes all semester. When math problems strike, everybody needs someone to share the misery and lighten the load.

But we do have tools for these special repair jobs, don't we, Lord? The quick hug for a discouraged teen that says, "I love you. I'm proud of you. I have faith in you." Perhaps that gives him the courage to retain his own values, to go against the crowd, to do what he knows is right.

We have the gift of silence, to sit with someone for whom there are no words to heal a hurt. Then that loving silence acts as a balm, soothes the spirit, restores the aching heart. Some people might call it acceptance or psychological support, but we parents know it by its true name—love. We share the hurt, we shoulder part of the pain, we refuse to diminish genuine suffering with a "cheer up, things could be worse" pep talk. And somehow, by keeping faithful silence with our children, we enable them to discover for themselves that things could be worse. They might be left to hurt alone, without the gentle, silent touch of love.

In this job of family mending, there is a time for everything, Father. A time to cuddle and kiss. A time to rock and hug. A time to walk together and a time to sit quietly, sending out invisible messages of comfort. There is a time to cheer, a time to cry beside a child wounded in soul and spirit. There is a time to dance, a time to leave the healing in Your Hands. And through it all, there is always the time to love. Each child, young or nearly grown, will never outgrow his need for that love. And it is we parents who supply it in abundance, in whatever form it takes.

We have acquired the items in our sewing boxes and tool kits to help us fix our children's things. And You, Father, have given us love, the invisible glue with which to mend the child himself.

Pablum and Potty Chairs

At the Drop of a Rabbit Test . . .

JOAN

"I'm fat," I hissed at myself in the mirror one morning, surveying my eight-months-along tummy. "Really fat."

"You're supposed to be fat," my husband commented helpfully.

I burst into tears. He left the room.

That evening, in an attempt to soothe my wounded psyche, Husband tried again.

"I can't see why you're so upset," he told me. "Driving home tonight—just as I was rounding our corner—I saw this really *enormous* woman in a grubby old brown coat. Man, was she huge! I'll bet she has quads at least. . . ." His voice faded as I held up a grubbly old brown coat.

"It's my father's," I informed him icily. "Mine doesn't fit any more."

"Now listen, hon," he began to stammer, "my windshield was wet, and you know how water magnifies things. . . ."

I burst into tears. He left the room.

Although charity demands otherwise, I have always loathed women who sail, sylphlike, through their pregnancies, donning tents only at the last minute so someone will think to host a shower for them. By the time my physician says "yes," I already resemble Kate Smith's younger sister.

It is, apparently, an unwritten law that a woman who normally cannot remember when she last ate (and cares even less) turns into a ravenous fiend at the drop of a rabbit test. I wouldn't mind getting out of bed two or three times each night to feed the *baby*, but when the baby isn't expected for six more months . . . well . . . It's also hard to form a snappy comeback when someone asks, "You're almost due, aren't you?" and you just found out for sure last week.

I also despise expectant mothers who stare blankly when I mention morning sickness. Doesn't anyone else form an ongoing relationship with the toilet bowl during those first few months? By the time this phase has passed, my physician has entered me in the *Guinness Book of World Records* for the most weight gained . . . lost . . . gained . . . lost . . .

The middle months are the best. It's fun to shop for baby clothes, and still personally inspect my toenails to see if they need cutting. The doctor is hopeful that the latest diet he gave me will definitely work, and Husband beams proudly whenever we enter a public place together. I begin sneering at unpregnant women and use that new-found physical energy for delightful novelties such as cleaning the house and setting my hair.

Then comes the last part.

Did anyone mention heartburn? False labor? Knees that have permanently disappeared? Maternity clothes too bad for Goodwill? The neighborhood cheers me with a shower, but its effects are only temporary. They're all so *thin*.

"There, there," the doctor soothes, as I weep into a tissue. "I won't weigh you today, I promise."

"Are you sure it's a *baby*?" I sniffle. "What if a great, giant basketball . . . ?"

Husband has practiced driving to the hospital 104 times and has our due date circled in fuchsia on the calendar. Naturally it passes uneventfully.

"How are you doing, dear?" phones a particularly catty acquaintance whose considerate children were all born three weeks early. I hang up on her.

It happens one night as I'm finishing a Dagwood sandwich. Just a faint feeling, soft but insistent. Ignore it, I tell myself, reaching for a good book. But it cannot be ignored. The inevitable, the miraculous, the impossible has begun.

And hours later we are together at last, Husband's glowing grin meeting mine over the downy head of a small, perfect stranger. Who cares about the hot flashes, the tired feet, the unending diet?

We have a baby!

What Is a Baby?

ANN

A baby is a very special person. He smiles when he's happy, cries when he's wet or hungry, and never grumbles, "If you really loved me, you'd know what the trouble is."

A baby knows how to revel in the joys of each moment. A dry diaper or five minutes' rocking time are treasured beyond the world's largest diamond. He understands what true tokens of love are and never asks, "Can I have a stereo for my birthday?"

A baby is soft and cuddly. He fits himself democratically into the arms of a doting grandmother, bachelor uncle, or teen-age baby-sitter. He welcomes any attention and never remarks, "I don't think I care for those horn-rimmed glasses on you."

A baby appreciates little children. He giggles at their antics, enjoys viewing their activities, watches their every movement. He concentrates on each of them without making judgments on best or worst performance and never says, "Don't bother me now, I'm busy."

A baby enjoys an audience. He smiles and coos and waves his tiny fists wildly when grammar school siblings talk to him. He puts all his energy into his side of the conversation. He responds fully to the other person and never threatens, "If I can't be the pitcher, I'm going to go home."

A baby understands teen-agers. He listens intently to them and captures their hearts as firmly as he grasps their offered fingers. His eyes are fixed wholeheartedly on their faces and he never advises, "Don't you think it's time you got a haircut?"

A baby welcomes the attention of the maiden aunt who's rather shy around most people. He turns his full charm on her and never inquires, "Haven't you put on a few pounds?"

A baby brings out the best in grandmothers. He sits enchanted with her slightly off-key lullabies, now rusty from lack of practice. He snuggles gently into her lap and never suggests, "Maybe you ought to have your hearing checked."

A baby is a companion to grandfathers. He agreeably settles down to view a televised baseball game or lively political debate and never mentions, "Hey, don't you think it's time you changed some of your old-fashioned ideas?"

A baby is God's gift to the world, His Promise that all will be well. He is joy, love, unquestioning acceptance, the beauty of the universe condensed into one small but perfect package. His mission is to bring light and laughter to everyone he meets. Then, when the moment's task is finished, he settles into the sleep of innocence where an invisible sign hangs on every nursery door:

"Miracles worked here."

A Place in the Family

ANN

There's a marked difference in parental attitudes toward the first, second, and third child in the family. Before the initial baby comes on the scene, heavy classwork is involved—Lamaze lessons, La Leche literature, Parent Effectiveness Training . . . It's a wonder first-time parents ever manage to fit having their baby into the preparation schedule!

Fortunately, life becomes a little easier with each subsequent child. A more casual attitude, a little laxity of previously unreal standards, some flexibility toward the Almighty Schedule make having the second and third child less of a strain on previously overburdened young parents.

To the practiced eye, it's easy to determine an individual baby's place in the family:

1. Every baby requires certain basic equipment, first on the list being a suitable place to sleep. So you:

a) remortgage the house and order the finest white French provincial canopied crib—including the optional handmade imported lace coverlet—from the Stork Shoppe; buy a matching gold-handled chest of drawers; redecorate the nursery in colors psychiatrists claim will foster early learning; purchase a sterling silver infant feeding spoon.

    b) empty out the bottom drawer of your bureau and line it with a clean bath towel.

    c) tell the dog to move over and make room.

2. It's time to manufacture the daily batch of infant formula. So you:

    a) repaint the kitchen; don sterile cap, gown, and mask; and assist Dr. Jonas Salk during his regular house call.

    b) swish the bottles through the sink before doing the family dishes.

    c) tell the kid the world isn't going to cater to him and pass him his meal in a chipped jelly jar.

3. It's never too early to make plans for your child's education. So you:

    a) use the extension phone in the delivery room to reserve a place in Harvard's Class of 1990.

    b) pick up a couple of nearly complete educational toys from the local thrift shop in time for his third birthday.

    c) let him chew on the cover of a library book.

4. Most newborns have a tendency to spit up while burping. So you:

    a) wear a surgical gown to protect Little Precious from any stray germs lurking on your changed-and-disinfected-every-hour clothes.

    b) try to keep a somewhat clean diaper handy that can be used on the other end later.

    c) dye all your blouses yellow to match the formula stains.

5. Comfortable, properly fitted infant clothes are a critical part of any well-planned layette. So you:

    a) tell the Stork Shoppe to deliver six of everything in sizes 3 months through Toddler 4, and order three more French provincial chests to hold the wardrobe supplies.

    b) have a rousing battle with the three-year-old over some infant stretch suits she is using for her dolls, and run them through a quick rinse.

c) pick up two 6X sweatshirts at the local thrift shop and call it a day until he's ready for kindergarten.

6. Healthy, well-bred, nicely mannered friends are essential to your child's proper social development. So you:

a) require prospective playmates to present three character references, two recommendations from clergymen, and a certificate from the Board of Health.

b) tell anyone who sneezes more than five times to go home and infect his own family.

c) stop at the playground on the way home from the hospital and give the kid a chance to play shortstop for a couple of innings.

7. It's important for the whole family to get out of the house together once in a while and expand their horizons. So you:

a) pack the portable crib, the portable high chair, an infant swing, the collapsible buggy, two cases of baby food, four changes of clothes, half the contents of the toy box, three blankets, five dozen diapers, and visit your mother for an hour.

b) grab an extra diaper and spend the day at the beach.

c) hop into the car and head for the West Coast, stopping at a public washroom every two hundred miles for a fresh supply of paper towels.

8. It's time for baby to have his bath. So you:

a) raise the furnace thermostat 10 degrees, sterilize his rubber duck and plastic fish, set out a new set of ultra-thick towels from the Stork Shoppe, fill the bathinette and check the water temperature with a floating thermometer.

b) finish the breakfast dishes and give him a quick splash in the sink.

c) hand him a bar of soap and toss him into the wading pool with the dog.

9. Giving your child all the advantages can be an expensive undertaking. So you:

a) use the extension phone in the delivery room to call the bank and establish a trust fund.

b) encourage him to pass around his piggy bank at family parties.

    c) call the news agency and inquire about their minimum age for hiring paper boys.

    10. Eventually any baby will have a fussy time. So you:

    a) cuddle him, rock him, and breathe a silent prayer of thanks for the miracle of love you hold in your arms.

    b) cuddle him, rock him, and breathe a silent prayer of thanks for the miracle of love you hold in your arms.

    c) cuddle him, rock him, and breathe a silent prayer of thanks for the miracle of love you hold in your arms.

The Nicest Part of Childhood

ANN

Father, sometimes I wish we could freeze him and keep him just the way he is. Oh, I know that two can be a difficult age, Lord, with its temper tantrums and tears and lots of "No! No! Me no do it!" echoing around the house. Who better than the mother of a two-year-old knows exactly how obstinate he can be?

But there's an innocent beauty there, Father, which obscures the battles over toilet training and surrendering that much-cherished bedtime bottle. I try to be quietly firm about the first, and not make a fuss over the second. It's not too difficult to do, since I've yet to see anybody go off to work with a bit of nippled nourishment in hand.

It's all a matter of priorities, isn't it, Lord? Just as it is with everything in life. Just as it is with somebody who loves a two-year-old. He's caught between the world of babyhood, where he was always secure in my arms, and that of an older child ready to make short dashes out into the bigger world. So my precious two-year-old contents himself with short dashes into independence, from which he retreats to the security of my lap, our latest clash of wills forgiven and forgotten.

95

I love everything about him, Father. I love the perfect curve of his small cheek, with much of its baby roundness still there, yet showing traces of the older child he will soon become. I love his spontaneous hugs and kisses, the way he clings to me when he doesn't feel well or wants to make up after a battle from which he can see no gracious exit. I love the fact that I am still the center of his world, which is the reason for his temper outbursts. Sometimes he feels the inescapable need to widen his horizons, yet isn't ready to move outside the yard without holding my hand.

I love the way he sits quietly on my lap when we go visiting, until he feels at home. I love his grin when it's time for a cookie or I get the urge to nuzzle his neck as I so often did when he was an infant. I love playing silly games with him. Then his innocent, starts-at-the-toes laugh bursts forth. I love sharing a bedtime story with him. He snuggles next to me, sweet-smelling from his bath, cuddly-warm in those funny pajamas with the plastic feet. I love our adventures with the Pokey Little Puppy, Peter Rabbit, and all our other good friends from storybook land. I love the way he clutches his beloved, tattered plush bunny as he curls into the tiny ball two-year-olds become when they fall asleep.

I love his company, Lord. I love having him perched in the supermarket cart when I shop for groceries. He calls my attention to so many things I'd miss if we hadn't gone out together. It is his sharp eyes that spot an ant parade heading for their sidewalk-crack home. He never misses a kitten sitting in somebody's window or a squirrel scooting up the taken-for-granted oak tree in front of our house. He sees the first tulip bloom in the spring, the first snowflake when winter comes again.

We've shared the wonder of rainbows together, standing in a summer's drizzle. And we've raked huge piles of autumn leaves into which he jumped with a merry whoop and holler. But the special joys of those seasons with a two-year-old will soon be gone, never to come again. Next year he will be three and nothing shall ever be quite the same.

Oh, Father, I know You won't permit time to stand still so I may relive all these beautiful moments of two years old. But please open my eyes during the short time we have left, when he is in this magic world between babyhood and childhood. I can't afford to waste a minute of it.

Then, Lord, together we will be ready to face life with a three-year-old who shall take over our house and our hearts.

Three-and-a-Half

JOAN

Why must she have her sandwich cut sideways, her milk in the *blue* mug, and exactly five gumdrops for dessert? Can anyone explain why she is terrified of dogs, ecstatic over kittens, and totally bored with goldfish and turtles? Paint sets are her favorite indoor amusement, but only if she can redecorate the bathroom walls, her toes, and best of all, her brother.

Maybe it's because she's three-and-a-half.

It's an honest age, at any rate. Last week at the bank, she asked a teller how old he was.

"I'm fifty-six," the man admitted proudly.

"Gosh!" She stared at him in awe. "You *look* a hundred!"

She is a charming and gracious hostess to all dishwasher repairmen, yet haughtily refuses to admit the little boy next door—because he can whistle and she can't. She likes pretzels, pink lemonade, olives and jelly, but only for breakfast. She needs her thumb and rag doll in the morning when "everything's scary"; that afternoon I watch her hang upside-down from the back yard tire swing.

Maybe it's because she's three-and-a-half.

Does anyone know why she loves to play dress-up with floppy hats and high-heeled shoes, but detests her own pink ruffles and leotards? Why she can deliver a devastating karate chop to a stuffed alligator, but bursts into tears if Mommy looks cross? Why soap suds are fascinating if they're blown out of a bubble pipe, but "yucky" if they're used to wash her face?

Is it because she's three-and-a-half?

She's certainly a girl of many facets, this mystery child of mine —Daddy's "rosebud," Mom's chatterbox-companion, Grandma's little honey, Brother's biggest headache. She's tulips and fuzzy slippers, and ice cream cones and stick-on bandages. Funny and cuddly—and sometimes incredibly loud.

Maybe I'll never understand the how and what and why of her. But the challenge is well worth it.

Because I love her. Because she's three-and-a-half.

And because I can't imagine life without her.

Crumbs, Crayons, and
Nerves of Iron

JOAN

If I had to make up a Ten-Most-Admired-Women-in-the-Universe list, our local nursery school teacher would definitely capture first place. Not only does she possess extraordinary tolerance, *savoir-faire*, and mental stamina but she seems actually to *enjoy* pre-schoolers on a continuing basis. Which, in my estimation, ranks her somewhere alongside the angels.

Over the years I've discovered that nursery school personnel share a set of common traits. Tact, for instance. Only a preschool teacher can inform an eager-for-news mother that "Virgil should really leave his wrench at home tomorrow," when what she would *like* to shriek is, "If your kid shows up with that lethal weapon again, lady, consider your tuition refunded!"

The only time I ever noticed a teacher's composure slightly awry was the afternoon I picked up the small fry from the church nursery; Priscilla Patient, several strands of suddenly gray hair hanging over her eyes, smiled tremulously at me and commented, "Class was a bit lively today!"

I learned later that both of Priscilla's assistants had gone home with bad cases of dishpan hands, only one two-year-old took a nap, a chocolate-milk fight had raged unabated for a quarter of an hour, and three children had raided the secret finger-paint stash. Apparently, what Priscilla was really saying to me that day at the door was, "Do you have any anesthesia in your purse?" or "What time is the next flight to Outer Mongolia?"

In addition to tact, preschool instructors are always abundantly endowed with manual dexterity. It takes admirable co-ordination to demonstrate the scissoring of a properly formed snowflake while simultaneously flipping the "Wonderful World of Oz" record and breaking up a tug-of-war over a naked rubber doll. Play school teachers are the only people I know who can diaper a squirming toddler and eat a sandwich at the same time. They also possess a keenly developed nervous twitch, which enables them to predict the precise angle at which a wooden truck will be flung— thus keeping their health insurance premiums to a minimum.

A nursery school teacher also develops a strong sense of fair play, which forbids comparing one small student with another. This can be difficult, especially when each class is bound to contain a Marvelous Melvin, the type of child who is painting in oils while my kid struggles to decode the color wheel. How can a teacher resist favoring Melvin, who, during cleanup time, swabs down the bathroom and spray-polishes the sink tiles, while the rest of the group lethargically tosses a few stuffed bunnies in the bin? But she manages.

"Your daughter is doing very well," Teacher told me loyally at my most recent helper-duty session. I glanced dubiously at my offspring, who was rubbing paste into her scalp, then focused on Melvin, constructing a map of California, complete with desert regions and freeways.

"That Melvin sure is marvelous, isn't he?" I sighed.

Teacher gave me a conspirator's wink.

"Melvin occasionally still sucks his thumb," she murmured.

It was the nicest thing anyone had said to me all week.

A nursery school teacher gives far more than her required hours of teaching time each year. She gives mothers a much-needed break so we can cavort freely around the meat counter, or just stare at our wallpaper and listen to the silence. She offers fathers a fond collection of lumpy ash trays and "I luf u, Dadd" greeting cards, to be proudly displayed on business desks all over the country.

Best of all, a teacher affords preschoolers their first comforting glance of the Outside World, where hugs, grape juice, and unlimited crayons offer an ecstatic taste of the wonders yet to come.

I wouldn't be a nursery school teacher for all the lollipops in a supermarket. But I'm tremendously grateful for her unique contribution to family life. Even though the class is presently observing "Know Your Fruits Week," and Daughter's fig costume must be ready by this afternoon. . . .

I wonder what Marvelous Melvin will be wearing?

I wonder if there *is* any anesthesia in my purse?

Last, but Definitely Not Least

JOAN

Experts tell us that the best years in which to become a mother are between the ages of eighteen and twenty-eight. Having celebrated several birthdays beyond this point, I was therefore a bit miffed when I discovered that the stork had me on his route once again. In fact, I spent one afternoon alternating between crying jags and staring into the bathroom mirror searching for signs of impending crow's feet or cataracts.

But I was wrong. As I have discovered since, mid-life maternity can be the high point of any mother's career.

Take my bridge club, for example. When presented with the novel suggestion that they were to once again become foster aunts, my pals swung into delighted action—searching their attics for outgrown baby equipment and maternity tops which did not bear faded formula stains across their middles. Donations became so plentiful that I eventually had to station a child at the front door on a full-time basis to accept the daily bounty.

One of the surest signs of middle age is the discovery that one's new physician (despite a collection of advanced degrees) wears a Class of '71 letter sweater, and prefers Sonny and Cher albums piped into his waiting room. Teen-age obstetricians, however, also have an extremely protective attitude toward older mothers and treat us with the dignity our position deserves. Mine never even *hinted* that I should watch my weight, which did wonders for my sagging ego (if not the other parts of me which were also sagging).

Once the baby arrives, a mid-life mother discovers yet another benefit—there is no shortage of nursery help in her domain. Every child over the age of two wishes to be the first to feed, hug, and show off Precious Princess. (A two-year-old wishes to stomp her into oblivion, but that's another story.) We did put a stop to the eight-year-old's Peek Concession (three cents a look, ten cents a burp) because it seemed crass to pass Princess around at sandboxes and baseball diamonds, but on the whole, her older siblings were a great help.

Since every kid in the neighborhood is also much older than a "tail-end" arrival, baby-sitters are also $1.75 a dozen. And a mother who is coping with arthritis and an eighteen-month-old at the same time needs all the help she can get. My sitters were exceptionally talented; they potty-trained Princess, taught her the alphabet, and introduced her to pizza when the time seemed appropriate. Meanwhile, I hung out at ceramics class and left my husband's office number in case of emergency.

As our little one grew, I discovered another psyche-boosting privilege: as the Oldest New Mother in our area, I became somewhat of an expert on 2 A.M. bottles vs. crying-it-out and other maternal traumas. While our preschoolers cavorted on park swing sets, I conducted class each afternoon under a shady elm, thrilling my fresh-faced audiences with sagas of hospital emergency rooms, sibling rivalry, and other treats still awaiting them.

Of course there are *some* problems involved in advanced motherhood. What do you do with a rambunctious four-year-old at a high school sports award night (especially if she's carefully eying the bowling ball display)? Should she accompany you to the church's morning discussion group (Subject: "Enjoying Your Peaceful Middle Age")? And what about family vacations—will Princess survive a tour of General Grant's house? (Will the *cus-*

todian survive?) Or should everyone else suffer through an afternoon at Kiddieland?

But despite minor upsets, a tail-end child can be a delightful experience. Having raised a herd of older children with the precision of a drill sergeant, a seasoned mother now discovers that it's much more fun to leave dirty dishes in the sink and go for a nature walk with Little Miss Five instead. Life, always so fleeting and precious, finally holds the moments needed to smell a rose, bake smily-face cookies, and cuddle together under a blanket of stars—gentle episodes that might have been missed, were it not for that very special Late Arrival.

And now I stand at the front door, watching carefully as she crosses the street alone for the very first time, waving her off into a world with ever-expanding boundaries, one she must travel without me. I will welcome the solitude, the chance to get organized, think an uninterrupted thought, conduct a conversation in peace.

But oh, my little tail-ender, the price for freedom is so very high!

A Kiss for Kindergarten

ANN

Tomorrow is the great day, little friend. In the morning, you go to school for the very first time. A whole new world opens up to you then.

How ready you are to meet it. You've handled the bought-especially-to-start-school clothes so many times in eager anticipation of the day you would first wear them to kindergarten. And you've almost mastered tying your own shoes, except for the hard part—making a bow.

But I wonder how ready your mother is for this new life of yours? If I could, I'd hold you back just a little longer, close to me, where I can control the influences on you, share all of your life. For I know what lies before you.

Tomorrow, when you take my hand for the walk to school, I will be the one who dawdles. "Just a few minutes longer," I'll tell myself, "only a few extra minutes to keep you all mine."

When we reach that big, big door, you'll leave me, anxious to join the other boys and girls in the kindergarten room. And you'll walk through it, as your brothers and sisters all have done, without a backward glance.

There I'll stand, wanting to shed a few mother's tears because another baby has become a little man. But I won't cry. I promise you I won't. I never have.

Instead I'll concentrate on being proud—proud of you and Daddy and me. Proud that we've made you secure enough, in these five years, to stand on your own for a little while, before racing home to share the news of the day with Mommy. How we've built so much security, I don't know. All we've ever done is love you.

I admit I'm a bit jealous. Tomorrow you will meet the ultimate authority. Soon you will tell me, with complete confidence, what has to be done because "Teacher says." I must surrender my position as the all-wise to that other woman who is about to enter your life and your heart.

No longer will I know all your little friends. Joey and Mike and Sean are old familiars in our yard and our kitchen. But tomorrow you will broaden your horizons beyond that yard, that kitchen, this block. Tomorrow you will meet other children I shall know only through your tales of the schoolroom.

You are about to enter a world which makes it possible for you to keep your own little secrets. You will master the art of making Christmas presents: the paper tree chains, the felt and glitter bookmarks, the orange juice cans you will transform with macaroni and gold paint to hold Daddy's pencils. And someone else's hands will help you do it.

There is so much for us to share this year, you and I. Over cookies and milk, you will tell me what "Teacher said" and "Julie did." And I will listen, eager to view this little world of yours through your eyes.

It's so hard to let you go, my friend. For five years, you have been my constant companion. Together we have surveyed the supermarket, devoured the dime store, puttered our way through the plant shop. It won't be the same without you, without your warm, trusting hand placed lightly in mine.

Tomorrow I begin a new life too. Back I go to the organization known as the car pool. Each Tuesday I will fetch you and your peers, then deliver everyone home safely. The rest of the week, I shall watch for you, waiting for another mother to bring you home to me. Then we will catch up on all that went on in school, a pair of old pals huddled closely over cups of cocoa.

Yes, I hate to see you leave behind the warm sheltered world of home and Mother. Tomorrow you take the first step of a long, sometimes lonely journey where mothers are not allowed to accompany their children.

Yet I will always be with you, as I am with your brothers and sisters. Love is a bond which reaches beyond the doors of schoolrooms, beyond the boundaries of neighborhoods, beyond distance and time and place.

In the morning, I will help you put on the red-and-white-striped shirt and bright new pants, then tuck a clean handkerchief into your pocket. And we will be on our way.

But tonight—tonight, for the last time, you are simply my baby. And I hold you close now, at bedtime, just a little longer, cuddle you just a bit closer, give you one more kiss before saying good night. In your excitement, you don't notice your mother steal an extra kiss.

I need it for kindergarten.

Look, Ma—No Hands!

It's All Due to Patron Saints

ANN

Most obstetricians' offices have a pile of little booklets on *What to Name the Baby*. But before any about-to-be mom and dad leap into an intense study of the Greek and Latin meanings for possible names for their coming child, they'd better bone up on *The Lives of the Saints*. Once a baby arrives on the scene and is equipped with his own title, his patron saint takes over. Then it's too late to do much but watch some interesting things happen.

When our first born appeared for labeling, Himself and I fought quite a battle. He fancied some lofty nomenclature to inspire our son for life. I insisted Number One be named for his father and Thomas Aquinas. Who could better take charge of a little fellow who, we realized at first peek, was brilliant and destined for magnificent accomplishments?

Why didn't anybody warn me that my spouse's patron wasn't the illustrious Aquinas, but rather the apostle descriptively known as Doubting Thomas? Two decades of marriage and nineteen years of parenthood revealed the Awful Truth.

Father: "Do you mean this bill for $19.32 is all for *kids' under-*

wear?" (He suspects I purchased some ermine pot holders for the kitchen and lack the courage to tell him.)

Son: "Are you *sure* you didn't wash my jeans?" (He knows I only tackle laundry that's been placed in the hamper; but hope—like doubt—springs eternal.)

We tried again with Child Number Two, a beautiful daughter placed under the protection of Francis of Assisi. At least this time we had the right saint. But why didn't anyone caution me about the eventual fruits of his sponsorship?

Daughter: "Mom, you've got to let me keep this little bird until its wing heals." (That night, Himself and I measured the "little bird's" wing span at eighteen inches, determined it was a young hawk, and shuddered whenever it hungrily eyed one of the dogs or the smaller children.) "You'll never notice it's in the house." (And I didn't, because I was too busy feeding her five baby rabbits every two hours, and directing traffic for the guinea pig, a pair of hamsters, two dogs, the turtle, six fish, and three tadpoles she'd saved from certain destruction.)

Child Number Three, after some quiet years, placed herself in the care of Elizabeth at Confirmation, since she admired the cousin of the Blessed Mother. But we didn't understand at the time she'd demonstrate the same hospitality which made her patron famous throughout the ages.

Daughter: "I told twenty-three of the girls they can sleep over here Saturday night, and Sunday a big bunch is coming for a barbecue." (Didn't Elizabeth entertain just one special person, instead of rolling out the welcome mat for the immediate world?)

When our second son joined the clan, we felt he belonged under the guardianship of St. Anthony. How could he go wrong with the finder of lost things to look after him?

Son: "Has anybody seen my gym shoes/winter jacket/homework/science project?" (Is St. Anthony so short of business that he encourages this little guy to lose things in order to need heavenly help finding them?)

The younger boys also show the results of their saintly patronage. Our ten-year-old, in the image of St. Robert Bellarmine, has a thirst for knowledge. But did that pious Jesuit ever stumble home laden with thirteen library books at once?

Son: "Today's the due date, and I can't find four of my books." (Did we goof and tuck him under St. Anthony's wing too?)

Steve seems determined to follow in the footsteps of the first Christian martyr and announces his progress several times a day.

Son: "Help, Mom! They're after me again!" (I doubt that the original Stephen earned his crown by provoking his siblings to the point of mayhem.)

St. Christopher may have been displaced on the official church calendar, but his namesake is trying hard to win reinstatement.

Son: "Gosh, Mom, you didn't have to worry about me walking home from school alone. I wasn't lost. The nice policeman told me exactly where I was." (It's lovely that St. Christopher stays on the job, even though he no longer has a feast day to himself.)

By the time we reached the end of our tribal line, we ran short of appropriate saints. Intense study of a list of sanctified Williams failed to turn up a holy bishop or martyr willing to adopt our youngest son. Then a friend observed him in full toddler tantrum and cleared up the mystery.

"You must have named him for William the Conquerer."

Now that it's too late to arrange for different patrons, all we can do is watch our offspring stumble and bumble their way to sanctity, with some heavily disguised heavenly assistance. Still, Himself and I finally decided there are some comforts coming from the patron saint pandemonium.

We can't wait to see what our kids eventually name their kids.

Good-by, Peaceful Days

JOAN

When I was a young naïve mother hauling four preschoolers everywhere, I used to dream of the day when my little ones would become self-sufficient. How nice it would be, I mused, to have offspring who could make their own sandwiches, tie each other's shoes, and handle bathroom duties unescorted.

My children have now reached this pinnacle in life, and I'm tremendously pleased with their progress. It's wonderful to have kids who have mastered the following accomplishments:

They can eat unaided, and they do—before, during, and after each meal, in addition to their 10 P.M. feedings, and any spare potato chips they can sneak into bed.

They can dress themselves, and what wonderful taste they display. It's either jeans, torn T-shirt, and raggedy sneakers, or a razzle-dazzle ensemble of striped shirt and plaid pants (to be worn to school on Picture Day, of course).

They can amuse themselves. No more "patty-cake," or stuffed crocodiles. Interesting forms of play now include hanging from dead tree branches, riding bicycles no-handed, and leaping off the high dive after they failed Beginner Swim class.

They can help with household chores. What fun to watch Brother A bash Brother B over the head with the snow shovel, or referee dishwashing squabbles. How impressively they pull the oven door off its hinges and jam the toaster.

They are finished with infant illnesses; croup and colic have fallen by the wayside. Trips to the doctor are now more dramatic, usually involving an arm broken while sliding into second base, or the restitching of an already-stitched head wound.

They can go on errands to buy bread when we are running low. They will bring home two bottles of pop, four candy bars, and forget the bread.

They can enjoy adult pleasures such as incessant telephone calls, and Old Maid tournaments. They will also lift weights to build up their biceps, but cannot muster the strength to remove dirty socks from the bathroom floor.

They can get themselves ready for bed, but consider it indecent to retire before 1 A.M. What stimulating interchanges result as Mom explains once again the purpose of a toothbrush, soap, and water.

Yes, it's wonderful to have alert, growing youngsters. But sometimes I can't help remembering those boring yesterdays, filled with diapers, playpens—and nice long naps.

When I'm a Little Old Lady

ANN

Then I'll live with my children and bring them great joy
To repay all I've had from each girl and boy.

I shall draw on the walls and scuff up the floor;
Run in and out without closing the door.

I'll hide frogs in the pantry, socks under my bed.
Whenever they scold me, I'll just hang my head.

I'll run and I'll romp, always fritter away
The time to be spent doing chores every day.

I'll pester my children when they're on the phone.
As long as they're busy, won't leave them alone.

Hide candy in closets, rocks in a drawer,
And never will pick up my clothes from the floor.

Dash off to the movies and not wash a dish.
I'll plead for allowance whenever I wish.

Stop The World . . . Our Gerbils Are Loose!

I'll stuff up the plumbing and deluge the floor.
As soon as they've mopped it, I'll flood it some more.

When they correct me, I'll lie down and cry,
Kicking and screaming, not a tear in my eye.

I'll take all their pencils and flashlights, and then
When they buy new ones, I'll take them again.

I'll spill glasses of milk to complete every meal,
Eat my banana and just drop the peel.

Put toys on the table, spill jam on the floor,
I'll break lots of dishes as though I were four.

What fun I shall have, what joy it will be
To live with my children—like they live with me.

Never Anything to Eat

JOAN

For some reason, I always assumed that only infants had to be fed every three hours. It seems like only yesterday (actually, it *was* only yesterday) that I bent over a hungry baby at 2 A.M. and murmured groggily, "Someday, sweetheart, we'll be done with this nonsense."

Not so. Unfortunately, my children possess this irrational fear that if they stop eating, even for a moment, they will keel over from terminal malnutrition or some equally damaging malady. While other homes live with the constant noise of a blaring TV, a thumping dishwasher, or a whining toddler, our abode's most distinctive background feature is the steady sound of chewing.

The crunching begins before I lift my sleepy head from the pillow. My impatient brood is already consuming a breakfast that even Paul Bunyan would find challenging. They must fortify themselves, of course, for the long haul till school recess (our school has not yet instituted a regular morning student cocoa break). Sliding through a morass of egg shells and orange peels, I proceed to the chore of lunch-making.

117

"I only need two sandwiches today, Mom—it's Hot Dog Day," Second Boy points out.

"Boy, there's never anything to eat around here," Eldest Son welcomes me, looking up from his two-foot-high stack of french toast.

Mr. Second-Grader peers at the plastic bags. "How come I only get six cookies today?"

Staggering under the weight of their lunch sacks, the quartet exits. Third Son will consume his entire meal en route to patrol boy duty, hence will return home at noon, but the others will manage to crawl through the day, a mental picture of our refrigerator sustaining them during their darkest hours. For the time being, Daughter is the only food-a-holic with whom to be bargained.

And bargain I must. A piece of toast (her third of the morning) will substitute for the dill pickle she's screaming for (there's something indecent about eating garlic at 9 A.M.). A bowl of soup at 10:30 may tide her over till noon lunch.

But the real decisions come when I bake the daily batch of goodies. Where should I hide them today—behind the clothes drier or under the buffet? I gave up buying cookies in 1970, since a box lasted about five minutes, but the homemade variety can be somewhat controlled if carried directly from the oven to a combination safe.

At three-thirty the school kids reappear, and the chomping chorus echoes throughout our domain.

"Boy, there's never anything to eat around here." Eldest Son hangs on the refrigerator door. (Husband is considering installing a walk-in refrigerator for this child—there will be a hook at the entrance to hold his jacket, so he may be comfortable as he browses.)

Hopefully, Husband will also remember to bring home the small grocery order I requested this morning: five gallons of milk and one sow. Otherwise, dinner will be a dismal affair, limited to only six courses.

"Boy, there's never anything to eat around here." Eldest Son gloomily studies the cabinets (stocked only this morning) while the rest of us clear away the supper dishes. Daughter is wrestled into bed, screaming in vain for another slice of pot roast. The children hop on their bikes for the nightly journey to the corner candy store; homework must be fortified with nourishment, of course.

Two hours later, the last candy wrapper crackle has subsided, and little jaws have quieted at last. But my work is not yet ended. Like our infants, Husband will yawn and stretch at the stroke of 10 P.M. and ask, "Is there anything to eat around here?"

You can understand why I continue to buy a state lottery ticket each week. If we ever win the grand prize, I figure it will just about cover a steak dinner for our gang.

The Most Important
School Rule Is . . .

ANN

Law, like beauty, seems to be confined to the eye of the beholder. When our parish school board recently reviewed its policy on discipline, the principal undertook a survey of the students. She tried to determine what the children thought the school's rules and regulations were.

Principal, pastor, faculty, school board members, and parents are only beginning to emerge from the collective stupor into which we fell on seeing the results.

Our problem? We're not kids any more and don't *really* understand the child's point of view. We see only the obvious, and it staggers us.

Among the first-grade regulations was the edifying, "Don't fool around in church." I was amazed by the reverential feel to this one, constructed by a child on his way to instant sanctity or an early vocation. Until the principal mentioned my son had defined it, that is.

"You mean the one who stretches out on the pew and kicks his brothers every Sunday?" I asked. "When he isn't rolling his dime under the kneeler, of course."

"That's the one," she grinned. And left me to lurch home with a copy of the survey results.

Some of the child-established rules raise more questions than they answer. The second grade must be having a lot of fun no one knows about. "No spitting over the railing," was the treasure from their ranks. Has it led to much under-the-rail spitting? Who was the long-distance champ from the third floor? What else are they doing for recreation?

Some third-graders must have suffered traumatic experiences. "Do not talk to Terry" projects the painful learning experience of someone who did and found the error of his ways pointed out to him rather forcefully. But we can't find this particular admonition listed in the parents' handbook of school rules and regulations. Neither does it cover "Do not play with Donald or Ricky." Hopefully, next year's handbook will correct this oversight, and specify which students it *is* permissible to play with and talk to.

In a valiant effort to lessen urban noise pollution, the third grade strongly recommends to one and all, "Do not scream in the bathroom." But what goes on in the halls? Or doesn't their jurisdiction extend that far?

Fortunately, the fourth grade leaped into the gap, providing us with "No screaming in the building," for which we are grateful. Now we would appreciate knowing whether it was painful experience or enviable foresight that inspired one of them to direct, "Don't stop and tie your lace until you reach the bottom of the stairs."

Parental instinct indicates it was not the most popular fourth-grader who formulated the conscientious directive, "To report others." That honor goes to a student easy to recognize: the most bruised. And how much classwork is done by this vigilant soul, whose entire day is given over to the constant search for sin?

"Don't leave paper on the floor; it might catch on fire" could have been expounded by Smokey the Bear, were he currently enrolled in our fourth grade. Whether tidiness or fire prevention is the main motive behind this instruction is still somewhat hazy.

Stop The World . . . Our Gerbils Are Loose!

I have a hunch it was one of my own darlings who dictated, "No getting up from your seat unless it is an emergency or unless your teacher comes for you." He would interpret his teacher coming for him, blood in her eyes and steam pouring from both ears, as a definite emergency which called for a rapid departure from his chair.

Last winter's tonsillitis epidemic spawned, "No candy unless you have a sore throat and you need something to soothe it." Is it medically possible for the entire class to have simultaneous sore throats, triggered by a peer with a bag of lemon drops? Doctors at the Mayo Clinic might do well to investigate this fifth-grade phenomenon.

What is the penalty in the discipline code for disregarding "Don't trip going down the stairs"? Is there a monitor at the bottom writing demerit slips for the clumsy culprit as he lands and bounces twice? Has any thought been given to an equal rights clause for those inclined to trip while ascending the stairs?

This group has a very selective, strict moral code. "Don't rip off pencil cases" is as selective as a fifth-grader can possibly get. So is "No name calling on racial discrimination." Unfortunately, it's going to take some time to determine whether it is the discriminator whom the students are forbidden to call names, or the discriminatee. Could it be that there is a ban on racial slurs, while all other insults are just dandy?

By sixth grade, our scholars have become even more legalistic. "No kids can come back in the building after they walked out already" is witness to this developing trait. But some legal expert might find a loophole for anyone willing to leave on his hands and knees. "Get an out of uniform or tardy slip when out of uniform or tardy," of course, does not leave much room for misinterpretation. However we are still wrestling with "Put on your dress when you go to school."

"Don't talk in the room when the teacher is not there" makes a parent wonder. What do they do when the teacher *is* there? "Keeping good hygiene in lavatories" is another mystery. Is hygiene to be, by school law, confined to the lavatories and forbidden to walk the corridors or visit the classrooms?

It was the obvious urge for self-preservation which led a "little kid" sixth-grader to propose, "Not to bother other people so the eighth-graders leave the little kids alone." And I'm anxious to get a peek at the child whose wardrobe inspired, "No wearing striped or polka-dotted socks."

As soon as they recover, the language arts teachers plan a search for the origin of "corsity" offered by several junior high students who were thoughtful enough to define it further as "politeness."

By eighth grade, the students seem to have a nearly adult concept of rules. But they still have a long way to travel in establishing proper priorities in penalties.

Before their all-day field trip, the eighth-graders set two penalties for infractions of rules during the excursion. Punishment for major transgressions was exclusion from the graduation ceremonies and receiving a diploma in the principal's office instead. Those guilty of minor sins would be put off the bus and their parents called to collect them.

As one mother of eleven pointed out, there was definitely something lacking in our offsprings' differentiation between major and minor punishments.

"If I have to drive all the way to Wisconsin and fetch my son from some roadside, I'd consider that much more serious than missing the graduation exercises. And there's no way he would live to graduate anyway," she vowed.

The mental gymnastics which produced this list of school laws are beyond us adults. Long ago we put the maze of a child's mind behind us. Obtaining access to it now is a baffling journey. Our quest for enlightenment goes only so far, however. We have unanimously agreed that we never want to know exactly what motivated the inscrutable caution, "No violating in the washrooms."

Hi, Mom!

JOAN

"Hi, Mom. Back from the store already?"

"I ran all the way. You know I hate to leave you kids alone. Something always happens when I'm gone."

"Well, nothing did."

"What's all this mess in the kitchen? It was clean when I left."

"Oh, that? Chris got home from work and had a few sandwiches, and some baked beans, and some cake. . . ."

"But there's white stuff all over the floor!"

"I think that happened when Brian threw a hard-boiled egg at Nancy. He missed, and . . ."

"An *egg*?"

"Well, she let his gerbils loose."

"Where's Brian? I'll give him a piece of my mind!"

"Sure you can spare it, Mom? Brian's on the roof."

"The *roof*?"

"Well, see, it's harder for Billy to find him up there."

"Billy?"

"Your third son. Billy has a bunch of water balloons, and Brian's going to be his first target."

124

"He is? Why?"

"Because when Chris and I were accidentally wrestling in the bathroom, Brian turned on the shower . . ."

"On my *new* shower curtain?"

"And Billy got soaked. He was wearing that blue sport coat—you know, the one you just bought."

"I think I have to sit down, Tim. Would you find Nancy and bring her in for dinner?"

"That'll be easy. I locked her in the garage."

"The *garage?*"

"Well, she took off all her clothes, and I didn't think you'd want her running down the street like that."

"Why didn't you just *dress* her?"

"Well, I would have, but all the clothes in the drier are still wet. There's a few rocks in there, and I think it's busted, Mom. Mom? Listen, Mom, stop crying. . . ."

"What's Mom crying about, Tim?"

"Search me. You know how she always makes such a big production out of nothing."

The Proverbial Mother

ANN

I'm the acknowledged biblical scholar on our block. Oh, it's not that I'm more religious than the rest of my kiddie-chasing peers. My scriptural leanings spring from childhood memories of my own mother, who fell to her knees at least thirty times a day, murmuring, "God, give me strength." Mom pointed me in the right direction. (Thank you, Mom.) But now that I'm busy with a batch of my own offspring, I've carried her fine example one step further.

I've noticed that the maternal population around here, like Caesar's Gaul, is divided into three parts: (a) those who find some kind of authoritarian support for their my-kids-don't-listen-to-me-anyway-so-why-do-I-bother lectures; (b) those who get their kids up, fed, and dressed early enough so they can send them to play at somebody else's house where that unfortunate mother is still searching frantically for a left sneaker; and (c) those who sit sobbing quietly next to their automatic clothes driers until they can get hold of themselves or their kids leave for college, whichever comes first.

Option A has the most appeal to me (probably because I can

never find that left sneaker myself)—and it works! Take yesterday, for instance (and I really wish somebody would). When my just-turned-teen-and-plans-to-snooze-his-way-through-adolescence   son wouldn't rise in response to my "Up and at 'em, tiger!" summons, what did I do? Did I scream, "Listen, you lunkhead, schools don't make house calls!" or a sarcastic "Have you decided to hibernate right through the eighth grade?" I certainly did not. Neither worked with his older brother, so why should he be any different? Instead I reached for my trusty Bible, kept conveniently by the cookbooks. (My soufflés, like my children, need all the inspiration they can get.)

"How long, O sluggard, will you rest? When will you rise from your sleep?" (Proverbs 6:9) I blithely called up the stairs. By the time he'd located the dictionary and checked the meaning of "sluggard" (sometimes I surprise him with a compliment, and he'd hate to miss one), he was alert enough to teach calculus.

Yes, there are a multitude of snappy statements hidden in the Bible, waiting for the diligent mother who searches them out. Somehow the kids give me a lot less back talk when Holy Writ spills from the lips of this mother. It adds a certain, much-needed authority to my everyday admonitions. The Book of Proverbs is definitely a gold mine for moms.

"When you walk, your step will not be impeded, and should you run, you will not stumble" (4:12). That's got a lot more class than simply informing my lazy brood the car's in the repair shop again, so they'll have to hoof it to school.

"Wisdom cries aloud in the street, in the open squares she raises her voice; down the crowded ways she calls out, at the city gates she utters her words: 'How long, you simple ones, will you love inanity, how long will you turn away at my reproof? Lo, I will pour out to you my spirit, I will acquaint you with my words'" (1:20–23). These particular verses get quite a workout as the opening statement to the normal parental remarks made every report card period.

"This is the fate of everyone greedy of loot: unlawful gain takes away the life of him who acquires it" (1:19). I find this quite handy when some sluggard asks for another advance on his allowance, without going through the obvious motions of taking out the trash or oiling the lawn mower first.

"Because I called and you refused, I extended my hand and no one took notice; because you disdained all my counsel, and my reproof you ignored—I, in my turn, will laugh at your doom; I will mock when terror overtakes you; when terror comes upon you like a storm, and your doom approaches like a whirlwind; when distress and anguish befall you" (1:24–27). What more appropriate statement could be made to the careless child who, after repeated warnings, left his new bike in the driveway, and now cringes at the approach of an irate father who just turned it into a pile of high-priced junk?

"Then you will understand rectitude and justice, honesty, every good path; for wisdom will enter your heart, knowledge will please your soul, discretion will watch over you, understanding will guard you." (2:9–11) This passage is tailor-made for commending the perspiring but jubilant fourth-grader who, after great struggle, finally unlocked the secrets of long division.

Certain verses give themselves up to direct translation into familiar family terms.

"The fear of the Lord is the beginning of knowledge, wisdom and instruction fools despise" (1:7). ("O.K., you guys, I know this is a holiday and you want to go swimming, but Dad said you'd better clean the garage first.")

"Then they call me, but I answer not; they seek me, but find me not; because they hated knowledge, and chose not the fear of the Lord; they ignored my counsel, and like fools they hated knowledge: Now they must eat the fruit of their own way, and with their own devices be glutted. For the self-will of the simple kills them, the smugness of fools destroys them" (1:28–32). ("Just wait until your father gets home!")

"For they cannot rest unless they have done evil; to have made no one stumble steals away their sleep" (4:16). ("Listen, I think we'd better set down a few rules for that next slumber party.")

"When you lie down, you need not be afraid, when you rest, your sleep will be sweet" (3:24). ("If you're going to invite Hortense again, tell her to leave her pet mice at home.")

"Put away from you dishonest talk, deceitful speech put far from you" (4:24). ("That's a fascinating story. Now tell me what really happened to Mr. Murphy's broken window.")

"The curse of the Lord is on the house of the wicked, but the dwelling of the just he blesses; when he is dealing with the arrogant, he is stern, but to the humble he shows kindness" (3:33–34). ("Be sure you tell Mr. Murphy how sorry you are about his window when you offer to pay for it. Then maybe he'll return your baseball.")

"Let your eyes look straight ahead and your glance be directly forward. Survey the path for your feet, and let all your ways be sure. Turn neither to the right nor to the left, keep your foot far from evil" (4:25–27). ("Drive carefully, don't forget to signal when you turn, and take it easy with the gas pedal. Dear, are you sure he's ready to take his driving test?")

"Envy not the lawless man and choose none of his ways: to the Lord the perverse man is an abomination, but with the upright is his friendship" (3:31–32). ("I don't care how late the rest of the gang is allowed to stay out, you're going to be home from that party by eleven.")

"Then will you understand rectitude and justice, honesty, every good path; for wisdom will enter your heart, knowledge will please your soul, discretion will watch over you, understanding will guard you" (2:9–11). (Remember, I said eleven and I mean it!")

"Observe, my son, your father's bidding, and reject not your mother's teaching; keep them fastened over your heart always, put them around your neck; for the bidding is a lamp and the teaching a light, and a way of life are the reproofs of discipline" (6:20–21, 23). ("And not one minute later!")

"Men despise not the thief if he steals to satisfy his appetite when he is hungry; yet if he be caught, he must pay back sevenfold; all the wealth of his house he may yield up" (6:30–31). ("If I get my hands on whoever cut that cake I made for the parish bake sale . . . !")

"A little sleep, a little slumber, a little folding of the arms to rest—then will poverty come upon you like a highwayman, and want like an armed man" (6:10–11). ("The news agency called to say that if you're late for your morning route once more, you're fired.")

"A scoundrel, a villain, is he who deals in crooked talk. He winks his eyes, shuffles his feet, makes signs with his fingers; he has perversity in his heart, is always plotting evil, sows discord" (6:12–14). ("I don't think much of that new chum you brought home yesterday.")

"Be not wise in your own eyes, fear the Lord and turn away from evil; this will mean health for your flesh and vigor for your bones" (3:7–8). ("You guys turn off that television and start your homework!")

"From the window of my house, through my lattice I looked out; and I saw among the simple ones, I observed among the young men, a youth with no sense, going along the street near the corner" (7:6–8). ("Well, pal, you've gone out to 'bum around' with your friends at night for the last time.")

"The fear of the Lord is to hate evil; pride, arrogance, the evil way, and the perverse mouth I hate" (8:13). ("Don't you *dare* use that kind of language in this house again!")

"On the way of duty I walk, along the paths of justice, granting wealth to those who love me, and filling their treasuries" (8:20–21). ("Don't you think it would be smart to cut the grass before you hit Dad for your allowance?")

"Trust in the Lord with all your heart, on your own intelligence rely not; in all your ways be mindful of him, and he will make straight your paths" (3:5–6). ("BECAUSE I SAID SO!")

When I've finished admonishing the sinner and instructing the ignorant under my roof, I find comfort in another section of the Book of Proverbs that might have been written just for me, when I've had a particularly bad day.

"The Lord begot me, the firstborn of his ways, the forerunner of his prodigies of long ago; from of old I was poured forth, at the first, before the earth. When there were no depths I was brought forth, when there were no fountains or springs of water; before the mountains were settled into place, before the hills, I was brought forth; while as yet the earth and the fields were not made, nor the first clods of the world . . . then was I beside him as his craftsman . . . and I found delight in the sons of men" (8:22–26, 30–31). ("Lord, I dearly love these children with whom You've blessed me, but right now they make me feel older than time.")

Daffodils and Daydreams

JOAN

When the summer sun burns, and dusty winds whisper hotly through the trees, it is our neighborhood's little girls who teach the rest of us how to live.

Our girls, though they can and do compete mightily with the boys in any given area, have that calm common sense which apparently knows when to say "no." Their brothers may whip themselves into exhaustion on a baseball field, mothers clean stifling upstairs closets, fathers guide the helm of a grass-cutter while wishing they were back in their air-conditioned offices. But when the blistering heat descends, our small females search for—and find—the most worth-while activities of all.

Things like running a lemonade stand, for instance. Who has not watched, with melting heart, a small girl setting up her first business venture on a shady front walk? Boys have no staying power at this occupation—they hang around only long enough to consume the products of their labor—but it is a girl who has the instinct to set up cups and napkins, find a cigar box to hold neatly stacked coins, mix the cooling drink properly, and serve it with clean hands. Dropping pennies into the box, I am reminded of ancient days when my sister and I gave up quarreling long enough to run our own stand. For at least an afternoon, we were allies, partners in our maternal objective of cooling off the neighborhood.

Then there are tea parties under back yard oaks and elms, complete with cookies filched from nearby pantries, and dolls of all types ready to share the bounty. A gaggle of small girls sprawl in varying positions—all comfortable—and discuss cloud formations, ant hills, and Life. They alone have time to dream, time to enjoy the rapture that is summer.

And what about strolling, that idle pastime of years gone by? Small girls have it down to a science. Ambling casually along an avenue, they check out (and report on, at dinner) an amazing amount of local doings. What's on sale at the dime store this week, the condition of the swings at the corner park, which house is having what tree removed—our daughters, in leisurely fashion, discover it all. If our wandering females also push small siblings in strollers, even more gossip falls at their feet. For what neighbor can resist the sight of a pony-tailed third-grader wiping the nose of a baby in perfect imitation of her mother? Before the small caravan has passed, they collect bouquets of daffodils, cold drinks—and enough local news to keep houses buzzing for a week.

Perhaps families regard small daughters with such affection because it is they, more than any other segment of life, who demonstrate the swift passage of time. The towheaded toddler of a few summers back somehow becomes a pig-tailed school-ager, wearing her new Brownie uniform with pride. Yesterday's jump-roping fourth-grader changes magically into a slim preteen, more interested in the newsboy than her schoolbooks. The bubbly highschooler who baby-sat so recently is suddenly planning her own wedding. As the rest of us stand seemingly still, suspended in an immovable time capsule, the years are stealthily stealing our daughters away.

And so, when summer comes, each of us pauses awhile to watch and enjoy the little girls in our care. Autumn will bring schoolbooks, time schedules, activities, meetings, and busy lives. But for now, daughters are still ours as, lazy and dreaming, they drink up each moment of their softly shadowed world.

It's a Doggone Shame

JOAN

"What would you think about adding another member to the family?" my husband asked me last Wednesday.

"I don't know," I told him. "Is our hospital insurance paid up? Can you fix the wheel on the stroller? Should I finish the ironing?"

"I was speaking of a puppy," my spouse explained. "I don't think we can hold out much longer against that youngest boy of yours."

(Why are the children always mine when they're doing something despicable, and "Daddy's little precious" when, apple-cheeked and smelling of bath powder, they kiss him good night?)

Husband was right, however. Youngest Son had launched a campaign for dog ownership some time ago, and our resistance was slowly crumbling under his relentless hounding (you'll pardon the expression). It was bad enough when he pasted a larger-than-life color photo of a beagle with glow-in-the-dark eyes over his bed. I had to wend my way through the room each midnight, collecting sandwich crusts and stray ping-pong balls while attempting to evade those mournful orbs that said all too clearly, "How can you resist me?"

The situation had worsened when Son began casually burying rubber bones under our living room rug and putting copies of 101 *Dalmatians* on the backs of our toilets. But the morning I caught him trying to stuff a stray golden retriever into the hall closet was the day I decided to face facts. It was time for a serious consultation.

"Just what do you have against dogs?" asked Son in his most impressive Perry Mason imitation. "Other people have them."

"I have nothing against dogs," I replied truthfully, "providing they stay in other people's houses."

"Give me one good reason why we can't have a dog!"

"Take your pick. First of all, we happen to have a baby in this family." I glanced fondly at our youngest, who was busily tossing together a chocolate layer cake.

"*Her?* She's almost five years old!"

"Well, I still think of her as a baby. Secondly, our yard isn't fenced. Who's going to explain the joys of outdoor plumbing to this creature at four-hour intervals every day?"

"Huh?"

"Who's going to walk the darn thing?"

He drew himself up to his full four feet of budding maturity.

"As the dog's owner, I will. Naturally."

"All right. Try this on for size. Dog food is expensive."

He eyed my ash tray.

"So are cigarettes." Honestly, some kids have absolutely no tact.

"I'll outsmart him," I told the family that evening at dinner. "If you offer a child a substitute, he may forget his original intention."

"Very impressive, Ma," said the high school sophomore, spearing the last piece of pot roast. "Did Dr. Spock say that?"

"Actually, Lucifer said that, the first time he tempted a kid into watching a dinosaur race instead of finishing his math tablet."

The next day I visited the pet store and selected two gerbils. Their superior attributes were obvious: gerbils do not make a habit of teething on leather purses and rarely whine at the back door to get in or out.

However, gerbils do have one major drawback, as we discovered a few weeks later when Youngest Son awakened us by dancing in the middle of our bed.

"Thirteen!" he screeched. "I have thirteen gerbils! If I sell each one for a dollar, I'll have almost enough money to buy an Irish setter!"

My husband buried his head under the pillow.

"Wasn't it Lucifer who said . . . ?"

"Never mind," I told him.

Perhaps what Son needed was a job to take his mind off this canine compulsion. His brothers were still delivering morning newspapers, so we talked the eldest into donating his gray sack to the Cause.

"It'll be just like walking a dog every day," Eldest promised the youngest, "only you'll have a paper in your hand instead of a leash."

"Am I supposed to be thrilled about this?" Youngest Son wanted to know.

"Just keep rolling those papers," Husband advised as he checked delivery tags. "Actually, this reminds me of my boyhood. Did I ever tell you people about my first newspaper route? Trudging through the snow, by the dawn's early light. . . ."

"You did," we chorused.

The beginning month of the paper route went very well. So well that Son earned eleven dollars, spent one on a giant bag of cheese chips, and banked ten for the possible purchase of a pedigreed Great Dane.

"Maybe he needs an expensive hobby," I told Spouse worriedly. "If he develops this bad habit of saving money, we're going to be in serious trouble."

"How about flute lessons?" Spouse suggested. "You know he's been nagging to join the school band. If he has to pay his own instrument rental . . ."

"And practice every day . . ."

". . . It may take his mind off this Fido fetish."

Son adored the fuchsia-and-maroon band uniform and practiced faithfully (once we convinced him that the upstairs bathroom was the only place that did his renditions justice). Of course, we had to have the piano overhauled so he could tune his instrument properly, and Husband took out a small bank loan to cover the cost of the lessons, but at least the expensive hobby was paying dividends. Or so I thought.

"Mom," Youngest Son asked me a few weeks ago, "how do you think I'm doing on the flute?"

"Very well," I answered proudly. "I find your version of 'Go Tell Aunt Rhoady' especially touching."

"That's good," he replied, "because I'm planning to invite all the neighbors to a recital in our living room."

"In our . . ."

"If everyone pays a quarter admission, I may have enough money to buy a St. Bernard."

Which brought us to last Wednesday, and Husband's question about adding a new member to the family.

"Well," I sighed, "maybe it *is* time to admit defeat. That kind of dogged (you'll excuse the expression) determination needs to be rewarded. Besides, I'm getting awfully tired of 'Go Tell Aunt Rhoady.'"

"Not half as tired as I am of rolling those darn Friday advertising supplements," Spouse pointed out.

"And did you ever dream that a gerbil's gestation period is so brief?" I asked him. "Yesterday I got three estimates on a new wing for the house. Maybe we'd better give in."

"I'm glad you feel that way," Spouse said, as he handed me a small box. I pecked over the top and met the dearest ball of beagle-colored fluff ever created. She grinned at me, and I grinned back. How could anyone resist those eyes?

"Welcome to the family," we told her.

Tomorrow I'll have to buy some birth announcements.

Everyone Else's Parents

ANN

Himself and I agreed the other night that there's only one couple in the entire world we desperately want to meet. Queen Elizabeth and Prince Philip can languish away in Buckingham Palace without our dropping by for tea. We've got no desire to visit in the White House either. Nor would we wish to join the jet-set beautiful people for skiing in St. Moritz, yachting to Monte Carlo, or any other fun excursions. They'll have to limp along without us.

No, our desires are a bit more local. All we want is an introduction to everyone else's parents. Because:

Everyone else's father earns $75,000 a year, half of which he gives his children for stereo tapes, Mercedes-Benzes to add a touch of class to the high school parking lot, and a few decent things to wear.

Everyone else's mother allows her daughters to pierce their ears in sixth grade, have thirty-two girls sleep over every Saturday night, and washes her own dishes. She wears a size 5 dress and always takes her daughters shopping to get their approval before she adds anything new to her closet—which she carefully chooses in colors compatible with their wardrobes.

Everyone else's parents take their family on exotic vacations every summer, never mention a part-time job for their children, and didn't have mothers who made them clean their rooms. Their vocabulary doesn't include the words, "When I was your age . . ." They never fret about report cards, never insist on homework being done, and are always thrilled to chauffeur the basketball team at the drop of a last-minute command.

Everyone else's father cuts the grass himself, takes twenty-seven Cub Scouts camping without a whimper, and bought his son a set of professional golf clubs for his eleventh birthday. He sets no curfews, makes no rules, and always checks with his teen-agers before making plans to use the car Saturday night.

Everyone else's mother lets her teen-age daughters paint their nails purple and her junior high sons grow beards. She never mentions baths, haircuts, chores, or taking out the garbage. She says yes to any requests for a puppy, a guinea pig, a pair of hamsters, garden snakes, tropical fish, and never inquires, "Just who is going to take care of this zoo?" She quietly feeds the fish, the puppy, the guinea pig, the hamsters and their multitudinous descendents, and never suggests, "Don't you think you ought to walk the dog and clean the fish tank?"

Everyone else's parents never suggest skirts might be too short, jeans too grubby, hair too long, pals too noisy, or allowances too generous. They're perfect in every way but one. Nobody's met them yet because they were recently declared a health hazard in our neighborhood and forced into quarantine.

Everyone else's parents make all of us normal moms and dads quite ill.

Psalm for Emptying Pockets

ANN

Father, You know how much I despise this particular job. Oh, it's not the labor itself—somebody has to do it, so why not me? I don't even mind the hours I spend cloistered in a dim basement on such a gorgeous day. Rainy days aren't any better for the task.

I think what gets me down, Lord, is the knowledge that tomorrow, next week, even next year, I'll be handling the very same garments. (We pass down a lot, don't we, from one child to the next, so outgrowing something doesn't take it out of my laundry pile.) But the worst part of all is going through these pockets.

Did You ever see such a collection anywhere else, Father? The kindergartner dearly loves that horrible-looking black vinyl spider with the stringy legs and carries it everywhere with him. Maybe his teacher despises it more than I do, but there's not much comfort in the thought. I hate the sight of it, and only Your grace keeps me from flinging it into the trash when I haul it out of his jeans one more time. Thank You, Lord, for strength. It's easier to live with that revolting object than with a brokenhearted little boy.

The older boys have moved on to bigger and better things, haven't they? The two-foot-long greenish-yellow snake that goes out in either the eight- or nine-year-old's pocket. How they love to fling it around! Our rubber reptile produces screams from girls, gasps from mothers, and limitless admiration from other eight- or nine-year-old boys. But it could be worse, couldn't it? The eight-year-old next door carries a real snake around in his pocket for company. Father, I wouldn't trade laundry-room places with his mother for anything in this world.

What is it, Lord, that makes young boys so fond of toting stuff around with them? Here's today's collection—broken bits of crayons, a length of string, part of an old fan belt somebody picked up somewhere. I can understand the cookie crumbs and candy wrappers —they're always hungry. But this non-edible junk puzzles me. It serves no purpose at all, except to fatten pockets and perplex mothers. What use could anyone possibly make of the top to a discarded ball-point pen or three links of bicycle chain?

Here are some things that might have been useful and helpful, if only they had reached me in time. Tardy slips from the other morning. I'm sure the kids left early enough for a leisurely walk to school. Did they become sidetracked by an extremely attractive display of junk on the way? It seems to me that must have been trash collection morning, when there are so many boy-type goodies to inspect on their way.

And the notes from teachers—the seventh-grader is behind in his math, the third-grader needs extra help with spelling, and I should have been at a parent-teacher meeting last Tuesday evening. Well, it's too late for that, but perhaps we can do something with all these undone homework papers crammed into the pockets of the ten-year-old's school pants.

Father, that's it on the jeans and school clothes for today. Time now to extract the underwear and socks from the drier, then fold and sort them into people-oriented piles. You've given me strength to face the contents of those boyish pockets, Lord. Please don't abandon me now.

Could You please work just one small miracle, and this time let all the socks come out in proper pairs with nothing left over?

Amen.

Oh, Mother,
You Just Don't
Understand

First Date

JOAN

You lean casually against the kitchen door, long and lanky, absently jingling the coins in your pocket.

"We'll be home early, Mom," you reassure me, waiting for the summons of a beeping horn, the chariot taking you on your first date. And as I load the dishwasher, the saucers blur before my eyes.

My son, my eldest, where have the years flown? The tiny white shoe, once so precious and sturdy, has given way to incredibly giant boots, now buffed to a high sheen—by you. Mothers do not polish shoes for teen-agers.

I stare for a moment at the corduroy sport coat, a duplicate of one hanging in your father's closet, and memories of other coats, small and proud, come flooding. Eton suits on Christmas mornings, red blazers and bow ties for Little League banquets—now just colored shadows from another time. Where did the time go?

Hour by hour, year by year, a little boy stole through my life—exuberant, polite, restless, thoughtful, but growing, always growing, always moving toward this day.

And I did not notice. Caught up in the relentless rush of laun-

144

dry, dishes, fatigue, frustration, I did not realize that time moves on. It will always be like this, I thought. My son, my eldest, will always be here. But it is not so.

For tonight you take yet another step away from home and family—moving farther into a world we can share only from a distance. I am proud of you, my son, proud that you are confident enough to take this step, proud and certain that you will handle it as you handle everything else too, with honor and trust.

But I am afraid, too. For there is so much you have yet to learn, things others must teach you, rather than I. Will they care as much about you as we do, these shadowy, unknown teachers? Will this new world, different and remote, bring you the fulfillment of our long-ago dreams?

The horn sounds, breaking our silence, and you lean over for a quick, shy kiss. Just an instant, but our eyes meet. And I see the face of my love reflected in yours.

"We'll be fine, Mom," you tell me. And suddenly, I know you will. For the child must grow into the man, as surely as day into night. As surely as time must pass, swift and unseen, toward the final letting-go. Tonight I deliver you into a waiting car, just as years ago we've said good-by at a classroom door, a school bus, an athletic field. It is never easy, son, but it is right. The best mother works herself out of a job one day. And you have always deserved the best.

"Have a good time," I tell you, and watch as you go down the walk and into the car, hurrying toward the unknown girl whose mother must be watching too. I watch until the taillights have vanished in the night, until the street is silent once more.

Have a very good time, my son. I love you.

Just One Big, Happy Wardrobe

ANN

My favorite blouse went to a party last night, and had a wonderful time. At least that's what my older daughter told me. Other people may have different ideas of social success. Being presented to the Queen at Buckingham Palace. Hobnobbing with the jet set on the shores of the Mediterranean. Schussing down ski slopes with celebrities whose pictures appear regularly in gossip magazines, on society pages, and campaign posters.

My social ambitions are much more modest. All I crave is a peek at the inside of some local hot spots where my wardrobe is already at home. That intimate French restaurant where my white silk blazer picked up those yummy-looking sauce spots. (Well, it's really polyester, but only the washing machine knows for sure.) The latest fun eatery where waitresses zip around on roller skates. (My new green dress had a lovely time there last Saturday night.) I yearn to be admitted to inner sanctums where someone will be sure to acknowledge, "Your face isn't familiar, but I recognize the outfit." Two teen-age daughters have paved the way for my eventual debut on the neighborhood social scene. Their favorite items from my closet already know the way around town.

When I was a girl, I desperately wanted a sister, someone with whom to share confidences and clothes. Much of my desire stemmed from observing the best-dressed gal in my high school crowd. This fortunate soul was blessed with a mother and three sisters, all of whom wore the same size. She had a full inventory on which to draw—five coats, innumerable sweaters, countless skirts, slacks in every possible hue. Never did she sashay out to a party attired in orange plaid blouse and midnight purple skirt, as was once my fate. (Three brothers contributed nothing but aggravation and snide comments to my social life.)

When our second daughter was born, I could scarcely contain my delight. At least our first girl would have a sister with whom she could share. Little did I realize, holding those two tiny, pink-wrapped bundles, that eventually it would be MY wardrobe they shared.

I haven't a pair of jeans to call my own, or an intact set of pantyhose either. My few shopping excursions (those for size 6X pajamas and on-sale sheets don't count, since they permit little room for creative selection and come under the heading of duty, not shopping) find me mulling over possible joint items. Will this pink blouse co-ordinate with Younger Daughter's plaid pants? How does that shade of green work out with Elder Daughter's favorite sweater set? Should I buy the dress I love, or the two-piece outfit my girls would prefer? Decisions, decisions.

Life with my own mother, the only other female in the house (unless somebody counts our faithful dog) never prepared me for these crises in choice. By the time I'd outgrown my girlhood Mary Jane shoes, my mother had outgrown a few things herself—all the duds that might have covered my growing bones too. We held joint usership to white gloves and costume jewelry, both of which she gathered from my drawers. (Honesty demands I admit to making a large dent in her nylon supply, however.) I can't complain about my daughters' acquisition of their mother's white gloves (which nobody, including me, wears these days), and their pierced ears prohibit any light-fingered lifting from my limited earring supply. But everything else is in mortal danger, since we share the same contours.

147

There was a time, however, when all my garments were safe from attack. During their junior high years, both daughters forswore dresses, skirts, and anything which might possibly be interpreted as non-unisex. The only member of the clan who had to mount an armed guard before a closet was their older brother. His sweatshirts and jeans (particularly the much-patched ones I prayed would keep him decent until payday) had special appeal. They also cast a critical eye over their father's haberdashery. Occasionally his best going-to-the-office shirts appeared at roller skating parties, shoulder seams gracing adolescent elbows. The only wardrobe immune to assault was mine.

"Horrid, Mom!" greeted my rare acquisitions.

Oh, those were the good old days. But time inevitably marched onward. The first high school social ushered in a whole new era.

"Gosh, it's nice to see the girls in skirts again," my husband commented. "They have terrific taste. I particularly like the green one Mary's wearing."

"You said it was too short," I reminded him. "At least when I bought it for myself, you did."

Several years ago, when the transformation from disheveled unisex to occasional feminine garb began, I tried to buy a few things specifically for them.

"That's awful, Mom!" greeted every effort.

I mentioned their disapproval to a friend, as I fingered some lovely rose-sprigged fabric I wanted to use for the girls' robes.

"But there's no point in buying it," I told her. "They'll hate it."

"Get it anyway," suggested the mother of a female trio, "but this time, tell them it's for you."

I took her advice (and several yards of the yummy material) with amazing results. Actually, I could have thought of it myself, if I'd recalled a battle between siblings the previous week. Each demanded, loudly and at great length, that *she* would wear a certain red sweater to the basketball banquet. After listening to fifteen minutes of verbal dismemberment, Himself stepped into the role of logical peacemaker.

"O.K., whose sweater is it?" he demanded in Solomon-like style, prepared to mentally sever the threads that bound, if necessary.

"Mom's," they chorused, and left him speechless as they returned to the fray.

So it was no surprise when I returned home with the floral robe yardage, ostensibly earmarked for my own cozy winter evenings by the fireside.

"How come you never get anything nice like that for us?" they howled. "You always pick the good stuff for yourself!"

Perhaps it's not fair to complain about their frequent forays into my closet and drawers. Both girls are generous to a fault (especially with my belongings), and have offered to lend me some of their most precious duds. I'll borrow these classic styles as soon as the right occasion comes along.

It may take a while to find someplace appropriate for a pair of prefaded denim farmer's overalls and a taupe T-shirt with the slogan, "Atta wayta go, Baby!"

All This and Algebra Too

JOAN

Mentioning that high schools have changed since the dinosaur era when Mother was a cheerleader is the understatement of the century. Remember the good old days when English, history, science, and math consumed most of a teen-ager's classroom career? If one was lucky and passed everything, one might be allowed to take a senior year semester of Chorus, or even more daring, Drama.

Not any more. Kids today must select their schedules from a dazzling array which include Cosmetology, Introduction to Flycasting, and Film-making. Physical education has widened its horizons too. Students at our school no longer sweat out a semester of volleyball, but can also indulge in skin diving, modern dance, or bowling.

I'm hoping my boys won't enroll in Persuasive Speech ("Study of the Process of Argumentation"), since we seem to have enough of that around here as it is. And their impending voice changes will probably render them ineligible for Advanced Treble Clef (1 credit). But frankly, the class in cabinet-making shows promise— at least it's one way of supplying containers for their golf clubs and CB radios. And Detective and Science Fiction may supply *me* with a large stack of Agatha Christie thrillers to enliven those long winter evenings.

I've also noticed that high school guidance offices have an updated image. In my teen days, kids sent to Guidance were regarded as terminal cases, merely going through the motions before their inevitable tour of duty in the local reform school. But current counselors' officers are pleasant oases, featuring rubber plants, aquariums, candy dishes, and wall-to-wall sophomores, all cheerfully debating the relative merits of anchovy versus green-pepper pizzas. When consulting a student's adviser for a review of his behavior, a parent will usually be told that her offspring is "far out" —a description leaving much to the imagination, but somehow more hopeful than a recited tally of times tardy, classes cut, and assignments missed.

Another welcome feature is the addition of classroom driving lessons. Young women of my era learned to handle a car in deserted parking lots on Sunday afternoons, while our fathers shuddered convulsively in the corner farthest from the steering wheel, shouted each time we stripped our clutches, and murmured, "Lord, have mercy on me" at ten-second intervals. Obviously, we passed our rules of the road tests only because of St. Christopher and the now-extinct breed of license examiners who pleasantly overlooked sudden lurches and bent stop signs.

Today's budding hot-rodder, however, initially practices his skills under scientifically controlled laboratory conditions, and then takes to the highway in a buggy with dual controls. Instructors, selected for their high level of stress tolerance, keep one hand on the braking mechanism, and the other dangling casually out the window, while grading the teen on entrance ramp fortitude and rush-hour language. I'd say it's a definite improvement.

As my kids are fond of suggesting, I really ought to "get with it." And yet, some aspects of high school life never change.

A generation ago, "everybody's" regulation uniform included white bucks and leather jackets; today's school parking lots are a sea of denim and lettered T-shirts. Yesterday's teens grumbled through term papers asking, "Should the U.S. Give Aid to Japan?" while today's students footnote, "Should Japan Give Aid to the U.S.?" Cafeteria ceilings sport familiar chocolate milk stains, sadistic math instructors still spring unexpected quizzes on Friday afternoons, and no amount of detergent will ever banish the stale-sock aroma in the gym locker rooms.

It may be a whole new world out there, but personally I'm not convinced. If everything is so modernized, then how come my high-schoolers echo my own long-ago comment when presenting me with their quarterly report cards: "Mom, before you open this, there's just one thing I'd like to explain . . ."

Music and the Maternal Breast

ANN

If I ever meet the character who first suggested that children should be introduced to musical instruments, only one of us will emerge alive from that encounter. But in quieter moments (like those precious school hours), I admit I might be unjustly accusing some poor soul. It's likely the suggester was childless, and the introduction meant to be something quite harmless. ("Johnny, this is a trombone. Trombone, this is Johnny. Johnny, say good-by to the nice trombone.") But this placid scenario never happened to me.

"Mom, I want to play an instrument," Eldest Son informed me one day several years ago.

"That's wonderful, dear," I responded, thinking of that nice Liberace. He doesn't have much time to race around in hot rods, appears the tidy sort who picks up his own socks, and has the reputation of being most considerate with his mother.

"What would you like to play?" I asked my precious child fondly, determined we'd manage to stretch the budget enough to purchase a flute or harmonica.

"The drums, Mom."

If I had been functioning properly, his musical ambitions would have perished on the spot, and the boy himself given only a fifty-fifty chance to recover. But maternal instinct failed me. I gave half-hearted permission for a secondhand set of drums to enter our lives and our basement. (It seemed sensible at the time, since his little brothers were beginning to act a bit odd—he'd been using their heads as a drum substitute for quite a while.)

"It must be nice to know when he's home," a kindly neighbor commented soon afterward. We were standing at attention in our adjoining front yards. A roll of drums had just informed us that some head of a foreign nation was either (a) being crowned or (b) being interred. The musical announcement had sent us flying outdoors to view the coronation or funeral procession, whichever, as it passed down our street.

Yes, that was an advantage of his drum addiction I hadn't foreseen. No longer did I have to conduct room-by-room searches for him during his in-residence hours. Even Joan was able to keep track of his at-home time—and she resides twenty miles away, as the music flies.

"We've got to move those drums somewhere," I informed Himself while rubbing a shin I'd whacked on the bass for the twelfth time in my futile attempts to hang some sheets on the basement clothesline.

"I'll tuck them behind the furnace," the Light of My Life promised. "Then you won't see them, so you'll never know they're there."

He was half right, although we discovered one slight flaw in the "never know they're there" portion of his theory. Our old octopus of a furnace served as a combination microphone/amplifier system. Not-so-dulcet tones were conducted through the heating vents to the furthest corners of the house. Now there was no escape from the beat-beat-beat of the tom-toms.

"Have you given any thought to running away from home?" I asked Eldest Son in desperation. "Just tell us what we're doing to make you happy here, and we'll stop."

Eventually my eardrums were granted a rest and recreation interim when he took up the guitar. I found myself whipping up angelfood cakes, refinishing three old tables, and antiquing a chest of drawers to the rhythmic strum and twang of strings. Life with a musically inclined offspring wasn't too bad after all.

Until this afternoon, that is. Then Second Son burst in with his grand announcement.

"Mom, I want to take up a musical instrument. How does the tuba strike you?"

Music may have charms to soothe the savage breast, but it certainly doesn't do much for us mothers.

And Never the Twain
Shall Meet . . .

JOAN

One riddle that psychologists haven't yet solved is why two children raised in the same household, with the identical set of parents, younger siblings, and family values, can turn out as different as filet mignon and horse meat. And as our two eldest sons settle into their mid-teens, we find their personality contrasts even more striking.

Our boys do have some traits in common, of course. Everything they eat turns into hair. Their clothes appear to be rejects from the corner Goodwill box. Their standard reaction to a maternal question is, "Huh?" (Or, during especially communicative moments, "Who, me?")

But the similarities end there. They might have been shipped in from different planets, so varied are their personalities and habits.

Sixteen, for instance, has participated in every sport known to mankind, and can quote the batting averages of the local Little League line-up as well as all World Series contenders. Fifteen, on the other hand, prefers to spend his energy blowing up the chemistry lab or constructing a bigger-than-life human heart model

(which he will display proudly on our dining room table. During Thanksgiving dinner.)

Fifteen's bedroom is a stomach-turning exhibit of empty cola bottles, dirty laundry, ankle-high dust, and revolving neon lights (carefully synchronized with the latest punk rock album). His door bears a cryptic message: "KNOCK. WAIT FOR RE-SPONSE. If no answer, go away and try again tomorrow." Sixteen's door sign, by contrast, bids a visitor to "Come In! We're Open!" When one does, she notices that Sixteen's golf, bowling, and tennis shoes are arranged in precision formation on a spotless rug, near a carefully made bed, under a collection of certificates proclaiming meritorious service in gymnastics and Español.

Sixteen will shower and blow-dry his hair at eight-hour intervals; Fifteen must be dragged kicking and screaming to the nearest mud-hole.

Fifteen sees no reason why he cannot sign up for calculus, biophysics, and advanced meteorology next semester. Sixteen's most challenging course is Introduction to Horticulture.

Fifteen will gladly conduct a discussion with anyone from the age of three to ninety-three, covering topics from the winning format for tic-tac-toe to the state of National Health Insurance. Sixteen restricts his acquaintances to those between the ages of 15.9 and 17.2 years, and his conversation gambols to girls, sports, money, and girls.

Sixteen cheerfully spends his part-time job earnings on rounds of golf, hamburgers, car insurance, and the afore-mentioned girls. Fifteen possesses a wall safe into which all valuables are locked, and no one has caught a glimpse of his savings passbook since 1974.

Sixteen's favorite pastime is an every-three-minute inspection of the refrigerator's interior, but we must launch an all-out search for Fifteen whenever meals are served. Sixteen looks down on his father by an inch or so; Fifteen wonders if he will ever be taller than me. Fifteen can play any tune one requests on the piano and make it sound like Carnegie Hall; Sixteen has not yet learned the location of Middle C. Sixteen is up with the sparrows each morning, but we must set off an atomic blast in Fifteen's ear (and tap-dance on his bedspread) in order to rouse him.

Handling teen-agers would be simple if they were all stamped out of the same mold. But they aren't, and the constant personality changes are enough to drive a mother into Intensive Care. Even worse is the thought of what she will have to endure when *Thirteen* starts high school. He wears out only his left shoes. He's the champion grammar school debater and insists on practicing at the breakfast table. His room is a stomach-turning exhibit of gerbil cages, bar bells, and Incredible Hulk posters . . .

What can a mother do to survive her challenging, frustrating, and thoroughly intriguing teens?

Just love them, I guess.

To Sleep, Perchance? No Chance!

ANN

Sunday mornings are an ongoing adventure at our house. It's fascinating to attempt identification of all the bodies strewn across the living room floor.

No accidents or explosions have occurred in the neighborhood. This is not an improvised trauma station pressed into service because of some natural disaster. Those comatose forms are the inevitable result of a tribal ritual of passage through adolescence—and my daughters' fondness for having friends "sleep over."

Recently these offspring informed me I'd been chosen "The Mother at Whose House We Most Like to Sleep Over." This honor results not from my charm or exquisite interior décor, but the need for a perch to support a group of deliberate insomniacs this weekend. It could also be partially related to my habit of going to the supermarket every Friday that makes my domain—and my refrigerator—so inviting any Saturday night.

"We had a terrible time at Maureen's sleepover, Mom," Daughter Number Two reported last weekend. "Her mother made us turn out the lights at 1 A.M., and her father kept yelling at us to be quiet until nearly 4." Thus does the modern generation define child abuse.

Those not yet initiated into the wonders of the sleepover party might be dazzled at the stamina of the pubescent female. I'm amazed at the stamina of some parents. Around here, we succumb to the depths of despair (and acute laryngitis) long before two. But parent abuse is legal these days.

Why do they call it "sleeping over" anyway? My observation is that any sleeping done before dawn's early light is both unintentional and disastrous—from the sleeper's point of view, that is. Such lapses in social control have caused girls to be drummed out of the let's-drive-our-folks-crazy sorority. (That's the one with an emblem depicting crossed curling irons against a tricolor bottle of miracle headache remedy.)

When I was a high school critter, we called them slumber parties. This was equally ridiculous, since we spent as little time slumbering as our offspring do. Some things never change.

Basically, all slumber, pajama, or sleepover parties are divided (like ancient Gaul) into several parts.

First, there's the moving-in era, when girls arrive toting sleeping bags, pillows, blankets, pajamas, stay-awake aides, and whatever darling outfits they picked up at the army-navy surplus store that day. (This emporium handles the most desirable haute couture in our area.) Accompanying these cargo deployment maneuvers are the usual girlish giggles, standard small screams, and other suitable sound effects.

Next comes the settling-in phase. Once all luggage has been stowed, the sleepovers fortify themselves for the coming events with soft drinks, potato chips, pretzels, popcorn, and pizza, the purchase of which has left this month's mortgage payment in jeopardy. Anything remotely nourishing is dismissed with the scornful, "Junk food!" Permanent household residents skirmish through the kitchen, asking for grocery status reports:

"Mom, isn't there anything to EAT?"

We then move into the settling-down period. Participants don their jammies (the ones with feet attached score extra points for high fashion) and sprawl on the rug. This calls for the banishment of domesticated livestock and undomesticated little brothers who hoped to join the pantry raids. The phonograph is turned up to maximum volume, so all can freely exchange confidences. Secrecy and deafness are thus assured. An occasional hysterical burst of laughter wins over the latest rock records and sends upstairs residents reeling onto the porch roof in a spontaneous fire drill.

The agenda then moves smoothly along to the trying-on stage. Out come the newly acquired tattered jeans and T-shirts embroidered with puce frogs. Each item is proclaimed "neat." Envious "ooohs" and "aaahs" arise in direct proportion to the degree of parental nausea brought about by each item.

But these young ladies realize that clothes alone do not make the woman, so they sweep swiftly into the reconstruction period. Out come the make-up cases and hair roller bags. Within minutes they have transformed one another into a science-fiction buff's concept of the Perfect Person from Planet Pluto.

Finally the quieting-down portion of the festivities arrives. It is announced when my husband pounds on the bathroom door, ordering all cosmetology students to abandon their pursuit of the body, face, and hairdo beautiful and "HIT THE SACK!" Once the sack has been hit, further admonitions float down the stairs. "Knock it off!" "Turn it down, you guys!" (Gender jumblings come easily to fathers in moments of crisis.) Even the time-honored, "I'm going to tell your mother!" has little effect, since they know their mothers are already thrilled this uproar is taking place under someone else's roof. Eventually we invoke the ultimate threat: "ONE MORE WORD AND NOBODY SLEEPS OVER HERE AGAIN UNTIL YOU'RE ALL FORTY-FIVE!" This brings about the desired silence, broken only by the sporadic close of the refrigerator latch.

"Do you believe there's a hereafter?" Himself asks groggily as the bedlam softens to a dull murmur. "There ought to be some reward for parents who survive a night like this."

"Of course there is, sweetheart," I assure him. "Hereafter all we have to do is grab a couple of hours' rest to recover some strength. Then we can have the fun of waking them up in the morning and hearing them howl."

Revenge is the nicest part of a sleepover for any parent. Although the kids don't know it, we also have our emblem. It features a long list of chores for them to do superimposed over an alarm clock set for 7 A.M.

Brave New World

JOAN

Dear Mrs. Ryan,

Please accept my apologies for not dropping you this note a bit sooner; actually our kitchen is being redecorated after a series of grease fires, and my pen and paper were inadvertently mixed in with the wallpaper paste. My purpose in writing is to thank you and the entire Home Economics staff at dear old North High for accomplishing the impossible—teaching my sons to cook.

Being a firm believer in an anti-sexist division of home labor, Mrs. Ryan, I have attempted over the years to inspire my four boys with the joys of creative cookery, but to no avail. Not one of them has ever progressed beyond pouring milk over his cereal—or his sister. It's not as if they haven't had a good example either—their father is an excellent chef. (In fact, it was he who first explained the purpose of an oven to me, loudly, soon after our honeymoon.) However, our encouragement has fallen on deaf ears, until now. Thank heavens for Boys' Cooking 101.

You cannot imagine how pleased I was when Second Son brought home that large sample box of heavenly fudge last Friday. It was truly an impressive sight, watching him share chunks of his homemade chocolate with the entire neighborhood, and how nice of you to send an equally large box home with every boy. I only regret that I was not able to sample any myself. I was so busy nursing everyone—remember that strange dysentery that swept through town last Saturday?—that the fudge had disappeared by the time I went looking for it. My husband claims the Health Department came around to fetch it, but he may have been delirious at the time.

Eldest Son, too, is profiting from Boys' Cooking, and actually prepared last night's beef stew. It was delicious, and I was finished with the dishes in plenty of time for the ten o'clock news. I am glad that you have decided to overlook that little episode with the chili. I realize that when a boy puts something on to simmer during first period, he should definitely check the pot again before eighth hour, but you know how forgetful these teen-agers are. Hopefully, our family's gift of a slow cooker may soothe the principal's ruffled feelings somewhat.

Actually, the entire males-only home ec program has stirred new talents in my sons. If they are not stitching my pantyhose shut, they are weaving spaghetti pot holders or ironing their own shirts. (You will note the ingenious scorch patterns appearing on every back.) But Boys' Cooking is definitely their favorite—and mine, too. I've always believed that turnabout is fair play, and why should we women have all the fun?

I certainly hope that this new drive toward equality extends also to the girls. Frankly, my daughter can hardly wait to get her hands on the school's new lathe, but since she is only three, I've told her she will have to content herself with our electric saw for a while longer.

In any event, I wish you all an exciting new semester! With warmest personal regards,

Mrs. A.

Good-by, My Little Girl

ANN

I'm not ready yet, Father. I haven't had time to say good-by. Yet there she is, wearing her favorite old jeans and a bright new blouse, helping her father pack the car. In go boxes of stuffed animals, the suitcases—everything she needs to survive away at college. And here I am, trying not to cry, wondering where the time went.

I need a little longer, Lord. We were so busy this summer, there simply wasn't time. We had lists to make, Teddy bears and kangaroos and rabbits to sort through. We had to plan, to pack, to spend hours on those companionable shopping trips when we checked to be sure she would have everything she needed. We remembered the shampoo, the hair drier, the dictionary. We bought sweaters, sewed skirts, chose the robes and pajamas and slippers she would take. But in the urgency of getting organized for today, we didn't have time. And I forgot to say good-by.

Now she's almost ready to leave. I stand watching her out the window and wonder. What happened, Father? What became of that incredibly tiny infant at whom I looked with wonder? Where is the princess in the pink silk party dress Grandma bought, who daintily opened packages on her first birthday? What happened to

165

the two-year-old who threw a tantrum when her beloved grandfather tried to help her up a curb with her brand-new doll carriage? Where are the little legs that struggled so hard to master the intricacies of the tricycle? They can't have taken her too far. The carriage and trike are waiting, dusty but faithful, in the back of the garage.

I don't understand it, Lord. Only a short while ago, the house was full of four-year-old girls, tea parties, hospitals for dollies who needed tender nursing to bring them back to health. The dolls and china dishes are packed away, but where have all the four-year-olds gone?

Father, I did say good-by once before, and it nearly broke my heart. That first day of kindergarten, when my little girl left to take her place in the outside world. But she was back a few hours later, bursting with tales to tell, experiences to share over milk and cookies. She was still cuddle-size then, Lord, and we snuggled together in our comfortable old rocking chair while she told me about her newly discovered world. The rocker is still in the living room, but all that remains of the kindergartner is a plaster hand plaque hanging on my bedroom wall.

What happened to the First Communicant, a dream in the white dress I made her for that most special day? She was so lovely, Father, filled with a joy that touched us all. The dress is tucked away carefully in the attic, but I can't find the little girl who wore it.

What became of the little Brownie in her crisp uniform, busy with plans and projects and other young Brownies? Where is the champion cookie-seller, who turned every relative into a willing salesman with her charm and trust? And where was I, that I didn't notice how suddenly seven-year-olds disappeared from this house?

How did I lose track of the childish pet lover who turned this house into a haven for injured and abandoned animals? What became of the rabbits, the lost kittens, the sick dog she brought home to nurse until she found a good home for it?

It's all a blur, Lord, for it happened so quickly. Junior high and cheerleading. Shouldn't there still be some gangly, giggling seventh-graders practicing their cartwheels and somersaults on the front lawn? Surely they can't have passed beyond the hurrahs and go-team-go's that created such a din. There hasn't been time. But where are the short pleated skirts and bulky team sweaters, the pom-poms that danced on their shoes?

What happened to the super-conscientious scholar who spent so many hours on her reports, certain that they would never be good enough? Where is the junior high student who tackled everything with an intensity that sometimes frightened me? Where is the ballerina, the gymnast, the member of the choir? Where is the patrol girl? The teacher's aide who tied so many kindergarten shoes and always found time to finish each bow with a big hug?

Then came eighth-grade confirmation and graduation, Father. A long summer filled with high school plans and dreams. All that can't be gone. Where is the baby-sitter for whom the phone never stopped ringing? The tennis player whose sports magazines overflowed our coffee table? The baseball fan who spent so many weekends staring at the television in easy comradeship with her team-following father? But we raced through another four years of high school, then prom and graduation. After that we had our brief summer of college preparations, and I'm still not ready to say good-by.

What shall I do without slumber parties, giggling girls, and sisterly warfare over the contents of their—and my—closet? How shall we fill the feminine void left by one whose lengthy speculations over dates for dances and who's going with whom made a cheerful clatter in my helping-to-get-supper-ready kitchen? What will replace shopping trips for just the right shoes, interminable discussions over just the right dress, and long sessions at the sewing machine with "How are you coming, Mom?" as background music?

How shall I manage to carry on bravely in the face of a spotlessly tidy room whose collection of stuffed animals have been taken to college as the hostages of childhood? What will fill the empty space where the infant, the toddler, the First Communicant, the Brownie, the pet lover, the scholar, the athlete, the cheerleader, the baby-sitter used to be?

What shall I do without her, Lord, this child of my heart? What will I do without those banging doors and the announcement, "Hey, Mom, I'm home!" I never realized before what an important part of every day that was. I never noticed how bubbly she was, how eager to share the good and the bad, the little victories and small disasters with me, as she had always done. Perhaps that is why I didn't notice the time slip past.

Who will listen now, Father? Who will care and sympathize? Who will celebrate with her over a near-perfect score on some surprise quiz, or lament a theme that stubbornly refuses to turn out right? Who will reassure her?

How much like me she is, Lord. Perhaps that is why we've always understood each other so well. Why we always knew, during those tormented early-teen years, how to make each other absolutely furious without really trying. Why we've needed few words to convey sympathy, love, the unspoken bond between kindred souls. Why it has always been a delight to share things with one another. Why I shall miss her so very much.

We've been through this before, haven't we, Father? Being a parent is really a lifetime of saying good-by. To infancy, to childhood, to adolescence. Time moved her forward until today, when I must say good-by again, although I would hold her back just a little longer if only I could.

And now she's ready to leave. The car is packed for the long drive ahead. Be with her, Lord, through these college years. Look after her, listen to her, love her—as You have always done. Be with me too, for I need Your strength to let her go.

Shall we go outside now, Father? It's time to say good-by.

If Only I Had Known

The Perfect Situation

JOAN

"Are you a working mother?" the voice at the other end of the telephone inquired.

Frankly, I always thought that *all* mothers were working mothers. But I knew what she meant—was I one of those who toiled Out There to gain fulfillment, a pay check, and a twenty-two-hour day?

Not so far, I'm not. But the thought crosses my mind every so often. (Actually, it crosses my mind every afternoon about three-thirty as the kids pile in the door.) It must be great to be paid for one's labor, to have one's social status rest on something more exciting than waxy yellow build-up. Holding down a job does wonders for a woman's psyche too, I'm told. Meeting other women in a competitive situation sometimes inspires a housewife to shed the extra pounds she's been toting around since Baby #2, and spruce up her outward image a bit. In addition, her self-esteem undergoes a metamorphosis as well. "I'm Somebody!" she can shriek to herself, even if "Somebody" is only Clerk #42, or "the lady in the invoice department."

Getting hired to do something at regular intervals on an unyielding schedule also makes an efficiency expert out of many a slob. One of my full-time-housewife friends was so disorganized that her husband used to host a neighborhood celebration whenever she laundered his socks. She spent her entire day going back and forth to the grocery store, since she could only remember one item at a time. But when she finally went back to surgical nursing, she became a whirling dervish, completing all household chores by 6 A.M., in order to be in her whites by 7. (Once she accidentally set the kids out with the garbage, but we've all done that, working or non-.)

As my friends, one by one, have sent their last child off to school, many have rejoined the outside labor force. Most work only part time, and if their new careers haven't upset them, they've certainly played havoc with me! Imagine trying to find a fourth for this week's bridge game when I can't call Kathy between one and four on Tuesdays and Thursdays, since she's tutoring this semester; Maureen can only be reached after three on Wednesdays and Saturdays because she's working overtime this month in Accounts Receivable; and Lynn can't come on Friday since she's catering a dinner party. Maybe we ought to play Monopoly instead.

Actually, I have to admit that the prospect of earning some extra cash does sound thrilling. After I pay the increased transportation, clothing, baby-sitting, tax, and Social Security costs, there might even be some left over to stash away for my fallen arch surgery. So that is why, a few weeks ago, I scanned the want ads with rising hopes. Surely there must be—somewhere—the Perfect Situation for me.

I skipped all the Analyst/Programmer/Electronic Technician/ Turret Lathe Operator items, since my mechanical ability is limited to pressing the defrost button on our refrigerator. Likewise the secretarial and bookkeeper positions—my education in Medieval History didn't seem quite appropriate. (It doesn't seem appropriate for the job I'm doing *now* either, but that's another story.) "Handy with Hair?" one ad queried politely. Only when I'm vacuuming it up, I told the ad, and continued my search.

But there was no Perfect Situation available. I found several jobs for which I was eminently well qualified, but being a short-order cook, school bus driver, hygiene inspector, or maintenance maid fell short of the dream role I had envisioned.

When I told my husband of this, my latest failing, he looked up from the editorial page in astonishment.

"Look for a job?" he gasped. "You can't be serious! Why, if you weren't here, this place would collapse into decay and ruin!"

I glanced around at the quite-obvious decay and ruin.

"I can't understand why you'd bother looking for the Perfect Situation," he went on, "when it's right here under your nose."

At this point, I retired to the kitchen to hunt for a box of crying tissues and a bottle of wine.

Upon further reflection, however, I have come to the conclusion that he is right, at least for now. What other job but housewife would allow me the freedom to stay home during a hurricane, get involved in an interesting morning discussion group, or spend all afternoon writing an article while the slow-cooker's aroma wafts through the house, my preschooler sings in her bubble bath (already a Total Woman), and the radio's "Moonlight Sonata" drifts across my ears? What other job offers hours of my own choosing (except when three kids will be late for dinner), the time to spend with special friends, the joy of an impromptu bike ride, or a quiet visit in church? What other position would grant me the pleasure of doing, full time, what I like to do best—caring, savoring, loving the most important people in my world?

There will come a time, of course, when most of these people will be home no longer, and quiet hours will be routine rather than a blessed surprise. It is well that we women prepare for this time, make changes in our lives to accommodate and enjoy this new direction. Perhaps someday I too will surrender my apron to the lure of the outside world.

But for now, it isn't necessary. Fulfillment, as I am discovering, cannot be supplied, or taken away, by outward trappings, positions, or roles. It springs, like most worth-while things, from within a woman's heart.

Knowing that one loves, and is loved, may well be the most Perfect Situation of all.

Playing the Energy Game

JOAN

In these energy-conscious times, more and more ways are being devised to conserve our natural resources and obtain the most from our energy dollar. But to be effective, housewives must be aware of these short cuts, and should be encouraged to use them. As a public service, I have devised a brief quiz, which can help anyone along the road to more efficient use of power and gasoline. Test your Energy IQ:

1. Your car will run more efficiently, resulting in better gas mileage, if you position additional weight evenly throughout its interior. If preparing for a cross-country vacation trip, you should:
   a) Stash luggage, tricycle, golf clubs, rabbit hutch, and spare tire in trunk; let Oldest Son hold Baby Sister on lap in middle of back seat; station other kids at window positions but away from soft drink cooler; keep Mr. Troublemaker in front seat with you.
   b) Stash luggage, tricycle, golf clubs, rabbit hutch, and spare tire in back seat; position children in trunk.
   c) Stay home.

2. Leaving lamps burning in unoccupied rooms can waste power. You should:
    a) Post a notice imposing fines on any household member who forgets to turn out lights.
    b) Follow husband and children around, reminding them of fines resulting from failure to turn out lights.
    c) Turn out lights and take down notice.
3. Your children have been home for two weeks with chicken pox, and you see your neighbor riding her bike to the store. You should:
    a) Leave the kids alone and offer her a ride in your car, thus doubling gas efficiency, and being neighborly.
    b) Leave the kids alone and bicycle along with her, thus getting some exercise, saving fuel, and being neighborly.
    c) Ask *her* to be neighborly by bringing you back a bottle of bonded bourbon and a straw.
4. Using your appliances at maximum efficiency will result in both energy and financial savings. You should:
    a) Remove marbles, candy wrappers, and pet turtles from heating ducts.
    b) Forbid the eight-year-old to warm up stale toast in your clothes drier.
    c) Limit your kids to one shower per week, unless their teachers complain.
5. Finally, develop a life style which eliminates frivolous use of raw materials. You should consider:
    a) Not eating, until the children grow up.
    b) Going nude, except for dinner parties and trips to the dentist.
    c) Putting your house up for sale, and staking out the nearest cave.

Scoring: There are no right or wrong answers to this quiz: its main purpose was to start you thinking about the energy crisis. If you have started thinking about the energy crisis, you have apparently passed the quiz.

If you can no longer think about the energy crisis, and are instead staring blankly into space and mumbling softly, you have failed the quiz, but you are reacting like a normal, red-blooded American woman. Congratulations.

A Not-so-secret Ballot

ANN

There's nothing worse than being a one-car family during an election year. Does the Republican or the Democrat get the back bumper? Who's stuck with the front one, which will be read backward in somebody's rearview mirror? And when bumper space is being handed out, are our finally-old-enough-to-vote offspring entitled to a few square inches somewhere to use for declaring favorite candidates? Solomon in all his wisdom never faced a problem like this.

Himself and I drive our precinct captain crazy, although he rarely gets a peek at our car. (The kids' political commitment doesn't extend to a boycott of any vehicle bearing the Opposition's label.) But he keeps coming to the house, since hope springs eternal. Anyway, he knows this is the place he can always locate enough kiddies to sport a dozen of the emblazoned T-shirts advertising his pet politician, or fill three front rows of the special cartoon shows for Junior Citizens that seem to be a Saturday morning feature at our local theater during the heat of every campaign. (I suspect he reasons that we registered voters will gladly use our franchise to support anybody who clears the small fry out of the house once in a while.)

We're totally apolitical when free shirts are handed out, but that too is a feature of our neighborhood. The staunch Republican clan up the street advertises its preference for a Democratic gubernatorial candidate on the ball field, while the Democratic officeholder down the block has fits when he sees his youngest dash about sporting a bubble-gum-pink elephant. Yes, the two-party system thrives in our community, judging by the sartorial splendor of the too-young-to-vote-yet set.

It's thriving among the voting population too, if we gauge by the window posters on the block. I take my morning coffee into the dining room, where I sputter and rage to see the opposition candidate grinning through my window. (He's the favorite of the household across the street, so they placed him larger than life-size in their picture window.) Can I find comfort in the fact that the same neighbors froth at the mouth when they back their car down the driveway, surveying our favorite in their rearview mirror? (We've got him, larger than life-size, presiding on our porch.)

Although our divided political proclamations may liven up the neighborhood a bit, things get far more lively within the family abode.

"Last night I asked my mom and dad who the best mayoral candidate is," reported one fifth-grade student to his social studies teacher. "But I still don't know. I couldn't hear their answers because they were making so much noise yelling at each other."

Junior high civics class offers a handy excuse for domestic bloodshed, cloaked in the more benign costume of concerned citizenry.

"Dummy!" hissed the Republican booster last night at dinner as he whipped the chair out from under an unsuspecting Democrat. (Are people this uncivilized in the mainly Republican suburbs?)

"Don't come whimpering to me when your brother-in-law needs a job," warned his opponent. "And it will be a cold day before your garbage is collected again." (Have we lived too long in the mainly Democratic city?)

When Himself and I later considered possible peacemaking tactics within the bosom of our family, we decided to ban all further discussions of politics at the table, in the back yard, or on the ball field. This remedy occurred to us as we watched two siblings who dwell across the street chase each other around with baseball bats, screaming, "I'll pound some sense into your politically dense skull." The younger generation simply doesn't know how to handle the political process properly.

Of course, if our children and their parents continue to show a lively interest in the mechanics of the two-party system, we can still work things out. All we have to do is buy another car and rent a duplex for the duration of the next campaign. It would be great to divide and conquer until the ballots are counted. Then we can get together again, to complain peacefully about whoever was elected.

At least we all share the same lively interest in that Great American Pastime.

Requesting the Honor
of Your Presence

JOAN

Maybe if Husband and I entertained more often, we wouldn't be tempted to stage an extravaganza every time a few friends drop by for an evening. Other couples don't feel obligated to repave the driveway or paint the garage in preparation for an indoor middle-of-winter bash, I've noticed. Nor do any of our friends go to the trouble of purchasing seventeen varying liqueurs, in case a guest requests a brown devil (crème de cacao and prune juice).

No, when our acquaintances mention "pot luck," that's just what they mean—dropping a pot of spaghetti in the middle of the table and having the good fortune to serve everyone before the tomato sauce runs out. Even better are impromptu family parties—the hostess can wait until all visiting kids have left before reaching for her scouring powder.

Unfortunately, Spouse and I cannot get ourselves into a "who cares?" frame of mind when issuing invitations. Since we entertain infrequently (it takes at least three months to recover from each Event), we reason that we ought to Do It Right when we have the opportunity. Take a recent surprise party for one of our relatives. . . .

"Did you order the brass band for the "Happy Birthday" grand march?" my husband asked me the morning of our Big Day.

"I thought maybe just a few tuba players—those kids from the next block . . ."

"Well, okay. How about the confetti?"

"Your sons are making it now. They're ankle-deep in the upstairs hallway."

"Good. Anything we've overlooked?"

"Just the food. I've been so busy restaining the paneling that I forgot to shop or make anything."

"Oh, well." He shrugged. "You can whip up a seven-course dinner in the next few hours, can't you?"

Over the years, I've noticed one glaring flaw among all eager husband-hosts. They have absolutely no conception of time or space limitations. How many hours will the chopping of one thousand celery bits require? Approximately what number of hors d'oeuvre trays can be comfortably squashed into a seventeen-cubic-foot refrigerator (without discarding chocolate milk, hot dogs, and other essentials)? How often will a preschooler's hands be removed from a crystal-laden table? Husbands have no idea—and care even less. That's the little woman's department. It's much more important, they reason, to spend preparty hours clipping the back yard hedges, so one's estate may be shown to best advantage.

Husbands also possess the annoying habit of compressing all the fix-it tasks they've been meaning to do all year into the ten-minute period just prior to the guests' arrival.

"What are you doing with that electric saw?" I shrieked one evening as Husband sent a shower of sawdust into the yogurt dip.

"Just shortening this table leg. You've been nagging about it since 1972. Then I'll take down that kitchen fixture and figure out why it won't light."

"But everyone will be here in a few minutes!" I wailed, pulling the toddler off the top of the china cabinet.

"You women!" Husband yelled over the whine of the power saw. "Always making such a big deal out of a little company. By the way, did you press my tuxedo?"

Another impediment to gracious entertaining is my own lack of confidence. Remembering my first party (which was so dull that even my husband left), and the second (during which our two babies escaped from their cribs and took apart the contents of fourteen handbags), I'm prepared for almost anything to go wrong. And it usually does.

"I wonder why the Smiths didn't come," Husband mentioned during a yard party, as he surveyed our guests throwing paper lanterns at each other.

"What did they say when you invited them?"

"I thought you invited them," I said in a quiet voice.

"Oh, swell." He glared at me. "Well, I might as well start the barbecue. Where did you put the charcoal?"

"I thought you picked it up." By now I was whispering.

Spouse sighed.

"I wonder what else can possibly go wrong?"

"Mommy!" the seven-year old bellowed at us from an upstairs window. "Nancy just threw up in the bathtub!"

Then, too, there's my reputation as "Un-cook of the Neighborhood," a distinction which, while true, is not destined to inspire enthusiasm among guests. Only my mother remains 100 per cent loyal—ooohing over a bowl of orange gelatin as if it were nectar from the gods. Our other guests, after saying farewell, usually beat a hasty retreat to the nearest hamburger stand.

Despite my desire to follow in Perle Mesta's footsteps, effortless entertaining will never come naturally to me. But that's no reason not to try—and try again. The warmth of hours shared in close companionship, the family's laughter echoing across the years, the small services to those I care for so deeply—all of these treasures make home gatherings fundamental to our enjoyment of life, and the people that make this life so rewarding.

And so I'll hitch up my jeans, make out another invitation list, tune the piano, try to remember the ingredients for brown devils, and push away the butterflies in my stomach. Time and experience have taught me that whatever else happens, several wonderful friends are sure to remark, "A bash at your house? Fine, but I insist on bringing a batch of goodies."

And that's *my* kind of party!

Needed: A Revolting New Image

ANN

For years the American woman has cringed while a poor wife hung her head in televised shame because someone peeked inside her husband's shirt and announced to the world, "Ring around the collar!"

Why can't some creative script writer carry this scene one step further by permitting the disgraced female to assert herself slightly? Women everywhere wait for the day the ring-around-the-collared wife turns to her spouse and bellows, "Why don't you wash your neck, you slob?" She might even recommend a terrific body soap manufactured by the same company that now points its "tsk-tsk" corporate finger at her laundry lapses.

This honest treatment would cause a Tide of housewives to Cheer, Dash into supermarkets across the country, commit All their laungry product funds to the support of this understanding manufacturer, and usher in a new Era of advertising.

It's not enough to lament the stereotyped wife and mother portrayed as a mindless ninny whose only concern is having the brightest wax/wash/windows on the block. Today's commercials end too soon. Adding a few more lines of dialogue, expanding the background scene just a trifle, could change the standard media pitch into a realistic product presentation which would find to-day's housewife panting with the overwhelming desire to offer her entire budget at the feet of modern advertisers.

When a ten-year-old boy comes in from a football session in the mud, wearing his best shirt, how about having his devoted ma wallop him before she reaches for the bleach bottle?

What can be done with the floor wax company that has come up with some super-duper ingredient that miraculously shields against imbedded heel marks and other kiddie-born grubberies? So far, viewers observe the user smile as she grabs for her sponge mop to whisk away the traces of their passage. A more realistic scene would have her chase the kids through the house, armed with that trusty mop, screaming, "I *told* you to wipe your feet. You think I've got nothing better to do than clean up after you?" That's a tableau to which any woman could relate.

Females eagerly anticipate the day when some genius will adver-tise window-cleaning compounds, a push-button-spray of one sort or another, by showing the teens-in-residence briskly rubbing at the glassy panes while Mom chats on the phone for a change. It could be the beginning of a new life style for families across the nation.

Homemakers have wearied of watching a modern husband lean heavily on his mop while he extolls the virtues of some miracle product. He's become an "expert," having taken over the weekly kitchen floor swish because his wife has gone back to work. But why doesn't he fill the audience in on more interesting details, such as who does the dishes, bathes the kids, and scrubs out the bathroom bowl? After all, anyone can stand there, gabbing and looking liberated, as long as he has a mop to hold him up.

And when that poor soul gets another headache, mothers yearn to see her reach for a hairbrush and apply a little child psychology to her noisy offsprings' backsides before she reaches into the medi-cine cabinet for tabular relief. Such an outlet for her hostilities logically follows the kids' use of the stereo as a deadly weapon on a rainy day. And it would send the entire female population flying to the nearest drugstore to purchase whole cases of the touted product, out of gratitude to a firm who UNDERSTANDS what maternal consumers suffer.

If anyone begins to write little bathroom love notes criticizing the average housewife's choice of toilet tissue, she would quietly switch his portion to some coarse grade sandpaper. Or invite the offending party to take over the management of her household pittance, provide the softer things in life, and still retain enough pennies to purchase some on-sale pot roast for supper.

When a teen-age girl pops out of the shower to start her litany of complaints with "MO-ther!" a real-life MO-ther would inform Daughter that, after using up a month's supply of shampoo/soap/deodorant/bath oil in three days, she can jolly well ankle over to the store and buy it by the gallon—using her baby-sitting money, of course.

It's time to revise the dishwashing liquid ads, too. Forget the lovely hands aspect, and get down to the main issue. Show the consumer several siblings fighting over whose turn it is to manipulate the dishcloth tonight. Then invent some clever way to convince them that, with the right stuff, DISHWASHING CAN BE FUN. It would be an educational experience for all concerned, and a true public service announcement.

Homemakers want to see more women giving instructions to their friendly plumber or appliance repairman about what *really* works on those grubby stains in the family sink/underwear/carpet. And, if some snippy deliveryman ever told a genuine mother, "Don't bother to show me the way to the kitchen. I'll just follow the path," she'd inform him he was well on his way to the teenager's room.

The day has come for realism. America aches to see the whole family manning and womanning the mop, vacuum, dustcloth, furniture polish, and non-phosphate detergent on a Saturday morning, because Mom holds down an outside job during the week. That would be sociological progress.

If this lofty goal is not soon attained, perhaps the American homemaker will go on strike until that TV woman is given the opportunity to talk back to her ever-loving family.

Then there would be true creative writing on television—at least during those long commercial breaks.

Farewell to a Faithful Friend

ANN

Furnaces are a lot like mothers. The only time anyone notices them is when they aren't working. One brisk fall day, the Heat of Our Home succumbed to terminal clog.

"I think we'd better get a new furnace," I suggested to my husband.

"Dispose of Lulu Belle?" he gasped in horror, throwing his body protectively in front of the aged hulk. (His hulk has been aging too, I've noticed, but can't match L.B. for size yet.)

"Shoot if you must this old gray head," he began to chant. (He's always had a touch of the dramatic about him.) "But spare this venerable monument for posterity."

"Cut it out," I cautioned. "That's the same routine Ben-next-door used last fall, and you know what happened during the winter." (Ben-next-door is ever cautious about the family purse—which may be why he had to replace not only his furnace, but also 497 feet of plumbing line when one followed the other to oblivion during a sub-zero spell.)

"Have you no sentiment?" cried my life-partner in one last desperate attempt to avoid bankruptcy. "No feeling of gratitude to Lulu Belle for the years she's kept us cozy?"

"Have you no memory?" I snapped back, growing rather weary of his far-off-Broadway performance. "No recollection of the time she cut out at 5 A.M., and you had to nurse her flue back into action in your nightshirt? No picture of those bitter wintry days when you trudged through waist-deep snow to check her oil tanks, cursing all the while?" (This last was a slight exaggeration, since the dogs faithfully beat the drifts down to hip-deep height, cavorting in front of their beloved master on his way to the buried oil tanks. He tossed them a few curses too, just for old times' sake.)

At the dinner table, he broke the news to our assembled troops.

"Well, guys, we're going to get a new furnace," he announced casually. "Your mother and I talked it over and agree it's the best thing to do."

"Get rid of Lulu Belle?" cried our eldest son. "That's terrible!" (Eldest Son takes after his father's side of the family.) "Where will I put my drums?" (L.B. may not move the heat around, but she sure conducts sound effectively—one of my minor reasons for wanting to wave good-by to her.)

"Get rid of Lulu Belle?" lamented Youngest Child. "Where will I play hide-and-seek this winter?" (L.B.'s imperial proportions have concealed 75 per cent of the neighborhood kiddie population at once—usually when their mothers are looking for them to do some odd chores around the house.)

A few days and several emotionally packed farewell scenes later, Lulu Belle's innards reposed curbside. Various family members descended into the void and viewed her streamlined replacement, now busy supplying warmth for our family.

"This is great!" said Himself as he surveyed her pocket-size successor. "Now there's space for the darkroom I always wanted."

"This is great!" said Eldest Son. "Now there's room for my whole rock group to practice down here."

"This is great!" said Youngest Child. "This winter we've got room to ride our skateboards, our bikes, our . . ."

Oh, Lulu Belle, I miss you so!

The Field Trip

JOAN

The bus is late from the field trip, Lord. I've been waiting here at
the park entrance, watching for the comforting sight of the large
yellow vehicle, chugging into view with its precious cargo of six-
year-olds. And it hasn't come.

We were supposed to be here at three o'clock, Father, to pick
up our little ones. I can still see their elated faces as they clam-
bered up the bus steps this morning, whacking each other with
lunch sacks, overjoyed that the long-awaited zoo trip had finally
begun. We were smiling too, Father, remembering day-camp adventures from years forever spent, savoring the children's excitement as if it were our own.

But it's quarter to four now, Lord, and the bus isn't here.

Strange how all mothers' hearts beat to the same rhythm. Anxious eyes scanning the horizon, we move together in a small protective cluster, as if this unconscious act could ward off the dan-
gers threatening to invade our world. Each woman's thoughts
travel the same path. Are they lost? Has there been an accident?
Lord, keep them safe!

Strange, too, how these moments of doubt increase our own

vulnerability, our awareness that we are helpless to control even the smallest detail, if You will it otherwise. And yet the thought brings a sudden rush of peace. For You are intimately in control, Father, watching the flight of the sparrow, noting each blade of summer grass, holding our children's hands as well as our own.

I glance at an unknown mother standing across from me, and our eyes meet. *It will be all right*, I tell her silently from the depths of my new-found courage. And I see the same certainty reflected in her eyes. It will be all right. He is watching.

Suddenly someone points, and the rest of us laugh and move away from each other, embarrassed at the intensity of our relief. For the bus is coming, Lord. You have brought our little ones safely home.

Thank You, Father, for this small lesson in faith, and for your never-ending protection and love. Thank you for our six-year-olds, who will enliven tonight's dinner table with rapturous accounts of giraffes and baby storks, giving glory to this triumphantly ordinary day. Thank You for mothers who can speak the language of the heart, sustaining each other when no words come.

And most of all, Father, thank You for a big yellow bus.

The Anderson Cover-up

JOAN

There comes a time in every housewife's life when she can no longer bear to enter a particular room in the family abode. The sight of faded walls, drab curtains, and an over-all film of neglect can depress even the sloppiest among us. Clearly, something must be done.

"What are we going to do about the bedroom (bathroom, hall-way, walk-in closet)?" I asked my husband one morning.

Spouse nervously folds the newspaper.

"What did you have in mind?"

"Either painting or moving to a new neighborhood."

"Fine, fine," he murmurs, reaching around me to grab his brief-case. "I'll get right on it."

Three weeks later on a Sunday afternoon, I broach the subject again.

"The bedroom (bathroom, hallway, walk-in closet) needs paint-ing," I announce.

"Who threw that pass?" Spouse yells at the TV sportscaster.

"I have here," I continue calmly, "a bucket of paint and a brush . . ."

189

"You can't just paint!" my Better Half interrupts himself in alarm. "The room has to be washed down, spackled, sanded . . ."

"Well?"

"I'll get right on it."

The trouble is, my husband is a meticulous worker. When he's finished decorating a room, the entire staff of *Better Homes and Gardens* kneels in reverence. His plumbing and wiring put any card-carrying union member to shame. His repair jobs will probably last right through the Second Coming. But he has one small flaw which dulls the luster of his accomplishments. He seldom gets right on it.

When three more weeks have elapsed, I turn to the children for help and usually find a willing work force. There is nothing more exciting to four school-age boys than the prospect of ripping apart a room and bashing each other with paint brushes. Since our work motto, applied to all mishaps, is, "No One Will Ever Notice," we are careful to tackle only those rooms not available to public scrutiny—mainly, the second floor. Areas that might be seen by outsiders are left to Spouse's superior, if somewhat sluggish, hand.

A typical recent project was the bedroom inhabited by Second and Third sons (and a host of other living things that I'd rather not mention). In danger of finding a place in the *Guinness Book of World Records* under "Most filthy . . ." the room begged for a face-lift. We collected our materials and assigned jobs.

Youngest Son was in charge of Baby Daughter, keeping her amused, clean, and alive at all times. Third Son and I would wash walls while First and Second boys moved all furniture and debris to a safe location (hopefully, the incinerator). First and Second boys would then scrub the floor while I cooked dinner, monitored Baby's activities, and broke up fights between Three and Four. While floors and walls dried, dinner would be eaten, Baby bedded, and dishes done. The five of us would then return to the bedroom, ready to paint.

Since Number Two possesses a rather peculiar quirk (probably inherited from his father) of using rulers to measure distance and mixing paint with a stick rather than just jiggling the can, he was assigned to any detail work. Oldest Boy, in training for varsity basketball, would paint ceilings (one leap at a time), and Three was in charge of keeping the radio rock station at highest volume at all times.

Actually, the painting progressed rather well. Although the walls resembled modified dart boards, Two had done an admirable job of patching, and Three had thoughtfully removed his football posters so we wouldn't be tempted to paint around them.

Our first mishap occurred when Baby Daughter, escaping from her crib, toddled in to join the fun and sat down in the roller pan. A sound spanking convinced her that her help was not needed, but the incident put me in a nostalgic mood.

"I remember that February when all you boys had chicken pox," I told them, wiping up spills. "I painted and wallpapered a room in one day and gave you seventeen baking soda baths, too."

"I don't remember that," said Four, painting his name on his arm.

"You were too little," said Two, "but I remember. That was the night Dad asked why dinner was late and Mom went over to Grandma's house."

"In a blizzard," added Oldest Boy. Ah, memories.

We were almost half-finished when the phone rang. In their mad dash to answer what turned out to be a septic tank salesman, two sons bounced off a wet wall and careened into a third son, who was at that moment touching up the trim around the wallpaper. Fortunately, the damage was nominal and offered us an opportunity to quote our work motto once more. (I quoted a few other phrases as well, but no one paid any attention.)

As we finished the last wall, a car turned into the driveway.

"It's Dad!" exclaimed Four. "Boy, is he gonna be surprised!"

And he was. His gaze went from polite to stunned to shocked to aghast to upset and back to polite. We stood awaiting the verdict.

"If you consider," I finally broke the silence, "that lamps will divert the light *away* from the walls . . ."

"Don't forget," Number One mentioned helpfully, "that the rug will cover most of those paint spills . . ."

"My football posters aren't even up yet," Three volunteered.

"Hmmm," said Spouse.

Later he reminded me that if I'd only curbed my impatience, he could have turned that upstairs stable into a shrine fit for Pope John Paul. I know I'm impatient. But really, I'm only thinking of him. After all, why should he waste his strength on a bedroom when I've already ordered the lumber for our new front porch?

A Lot to Learn

ANN

"Honey, you've clipped enough coupons—grocery, that is—so we can afford a family vacation this year," my husband cheerily announced one unforgettable day in the dead of spring.

"I'll make our airline reservations tomorrow," added Himself, who hops on planes the way other people catch busses.

"Why don't we just toss the kids into the car and drive to the East Coast?" I suggested with the aplomb befitting a veteran of the kiddie-to-school car pool sorority. "It could be very educational."

And it was. Otherwise I never would have learned:

There is a road across the entire state of Pennsylvania that does not have a single rest room. (It is easily recognized by frequent cries of, "But, Dad, I hafta go NOW!")

It is not possible for anyone to organize a family motor trip properly. (The evening before our meticulously choreographed departure, Himself and I succumbed to a bit of premature smugness. The car was packed, picnic food ready for the next day. Lists of instructions had been left for the dog-feeder and plant-waterer. Everyone had been bathed and shampooed. Clothes were neatly

193

laid out for morning. Our itinerary was posted with neighbors in case of emergency. Shortly after midnight, Himself leaped out of bed, screaming, "I FORGOT TO PUT GAS IN THE CAR!")

Our nine-passenger station wagon is more than adequate for our ten-person family (as long as we travel no further than the corner).

Long distance drives with children are actually composed of short-distance hops from one comfort station to the next (with background music furnished by the now-familiar tune, "But, Dad, I hafta go NOW!").

The six-year-old is prone to violent attacks of carsickness, which come without warning. (We discovered this unfortunate tendency before reaching the Chicago city limits—about the same time we noticed that no one would sit next to the six-year-old.)

Our fourteen-year-old daughter looks upon our vehicle as a sealed, self-propelled stereo system where no one is allowed to speak, but shallow breathing will be tolerated—barely. (She envisioned this trip as a 2,200-mile rock concert.)

A five-year-old, given the advantage of a side jaunt to Niagara Falls, is totally captivated by the wonders of nature. (So captivated, he spent all his time clambering over each massive rock like some Alpine compulsive whose bloodlines combine a dash of mountain goat with large amounts of human fly. Never once did he even glance in the general direction of nature's magnificent waterworks.)

It is not wise to take small children into roadside souvenir shops where breakables are displayed less than ten feet above the floor. (For bigger children, raise the limit to twelve feet. For uncoordinated husbands, make that fifteen.)

When family members are confined in a motorized unit for long periods of time, they get to know each other quite well. (This, however, is not an unmixed blessing. I realized, somewhere in Indiana, I actually do not LIKE any of my children. The feeling was totally mutual, my offspring assured me, in the wilds of upper New York State.)

The most beautiful scenery along the route is inevitably shrouded by fog whenever we pass. (Fortunately, we were able to find some lovely pictures in library books after our return, so we saw where we had been.)

I can't stand being near people who chew gum. (This revelation came simultaneously with the children's discovery that they are unable to forego such mastication without suffering severe withdrawal pains.)

The Ohio state police are very efficient and most polite when nabbing speeders (a virtue Himself didn't take the time to appreciate when cussing over his traffic ticket).

Driving is an inexpensive way for a family to travel. (Provided, of course, that certain costs are not included in the tally: motels, meals, auto games to keep the youngsters occupied for a few seconds, souvenirs broken in roadside shops, special cleaners to deal with the aftermath of the six year-old's queasy stomach, quarters to feed the motel's vibrating beds and pinball machines continually, and traffic fines payable to the Sovereign State of Ohio. There is also no need to add on the post-safari expenditures for family reconciliation clinics, marriage counselors, child and adult psychiatrists, or divorce lawyers.)

It is difficult to hold an intelligent conversation with someone whose sole interest in life is how soon she will be allowed to pierce her ears. (This discussion is the only one permitted to interrupt the twelve-hour-a-day radio concert.)

Never send an older child to fetch a younger sibling who is about to topple into the picturesque creek behind the motel, where Younger is studying the life cycle of frogs. (Younger remained dry. It was Older Brother who leaped into the trickle, emerging with three frogs and two tadpoles he resolved to keep as companions for the rest of his life, or suffer some serious psychological disturbance out of sheer spite.)

Rest areas by the roadside are only for resting. (The little notice, "No plumbing facilities," was only visible after leaving the highway with a twitchy bunch who were screaming, "But, Dad, I hafta go NOW!")

Eldest Daughter will swim only in fresh water. (This eccentricity was not called to our attention until we had traveled 1,100 miles to the ocean.)

Brothers who cheerfully share colds, socks, and beds at home will undergo a total transformation when placed in a motel room. (This is recognized by the incessant battle over who has the fuzziest blanket, the softest pillow, and the giant share of the latest quarter's bed vibrations purchase.)

The high spot of the three-and-a-half-year-old's trip is finding a knife at his place in the diner. (The low spot of a parent's is trying to remove it without triggering World War III.)

Teen-agers who win eleven large stuffed dogs at a resort carnival —but never capture so much as an ash tray at the carny two blocks from home—expect to bring *all* of them cross-country as proof of their prowess. (This created some interesting tactical problems, since the only item not returning home with us was one pair of the nine-year-old's shorts that had surrendered its seams.)

It is an excellent idea to check out all pertinent details regarding any tourist attractions in the area. (We decided to breakfast at a lovely restaurant in the Poconos. It had been mentioned in the motel guide to local points of interest. But the biggest point of local interest that morning occurred when we entered the door of that honeymoon eatery, and Himself grandly requested, "Table for ten, please.")

Yes, it was a most educational experience, although the lessons were not exactly what I originally envisioned. But our next vacation, to the West Coast, won't be nearly as instructive.

Next time we'll definitely take the plane.

Attention: Ralph Nader

JOAN

Dear Complaint Department:
Enclosed you will find one blue, long-sleeved man's shirt with a huge round stain on the front directly under the pocket. If you look closely, you will also notice that one of the shirt's arms is missing, but I am not writing to complain about *this*—it happened to be one of those non-returnable "seconds" that one often finds on sale, and I didn't notice the defect until I got home. My husband was not too thrilled about it, but he wears suitcoats most of the time, so . . .

Anyway, this letter involves the stain, which seems to be getting larger every time I launder it.

You will recall that I first called this stain to your attention when it was nothing more than an innocent blob of jelly, upon which I had used your SUPER-X stain remover. When the shirt came out of the machine, the jelly was still there, and in addition, your product had caused a large ring around it. In answer to my first letter of complaint, you sent me a large economy-sized can of SUPER-X and requested that I repeat the procedure. I did, the stain got larger, and I informed you of such.

Actually, your next suggestion was rather helpful to me. It had been a long time since our washing machine had had a thorough going-over—like most careless housewives, I usually wait until something is *wrong* before calling a serviceman. In any event, the machine checked out A-okay, the repairman had no idea what was causing the stain, the bill was twenty-four dollars, the stain got a bit larger, and I informed you of such.

My husband nearly put his foot down over your next suggestion, but he knows that once I am committed to a consumer problem, I will certainly go the distance. So he kept his mouth shut when I phoned our Bureau of Water and Sewers and had an inspector come out to check for rust in the water pipes. In doing so, of course, the workmen had to remove that portion of the house where the outside pipes meet the inside pipes, but you were relieved to know that there was absolutely no sign of rust or any dangerous chemicals in our water. Our builder is now putting the house back together, we have taken a second mortgage to cover the cost, the stain has gotten larger, and I have informed you of such.

Which brings us to today's letter. Frankly, I think your most recent suggestion is a bit much. My husband does *not* intend to wear a large, terrycloth bib at mealtimes, even if you do volunteer to supply same. Furthermore, the jelly stain was not even his fault to begin with—my three-year-old daughter happened to be making sandwiches for five of her friends, my husband stepped in to take the carving knife away from her, and, well, accidents do happen.

At this point, I can see no solution other than to send the shirt to your laboratory for inspection. Surely someone there should be able to figure out why SUPER-X is causing my shirt (and my marriage) to fall apart.

Please be advised that I expect satisfaction on this matter, or I shall be forced to contact my attorney. And if he refuses to return my call—there's always Ralph Nader.

Sincerely,
Mrs. A.

Nothing Like a Good, Healthy Virus

JOAN

Like most men, my husband would re enlist in the Army (and even volunteer for KP duty) before willingly mentioning the condition of his inner parts to anyone. I suspect his aversion to doctors' offices springs not only from typical suffer-in-silence male ego, but also the acute embarrassment he would undergo if forced to reveal certain details.

Women, on the other hand, have no such inhibitions. Our health records are an open book, available for neighborhood scrutiny and discussion at the drop of a surgical glove. And the juicier the details, the better.

"Gosh, it seems like the whole world's falling apart," I pointed out to my spouse last week. "Maureen just had her veins stripped, my sister Sue has a kidney infection, and poor Dorie is scheduled to have three wisdom teeth pulled—maybe four, if one is impacted."

My husband shuddered.

"Don't you women ever talk about decent things any more, like a new recipe for carrot casserole? My mother would never have *dreamed* of discussing her wisdom teeth with anyone. . . ."

"That's because your mother always had a new twenty-four-hour labor to describe at Canasta Club," I explained. "Eight deliveries should have given her . . . let's see . . . at least twelve years' worth of conversation. Who needs wisdom teeth with *that* kind of material?"

"But it's ridiculous!" Spouse persisted. "Shouldn't some things remain personal?"

"Certainly," I agreed, "and you'll never catch me blabbing about the state of your underwear. But a woman never knows when she may be asked to choose between local and general anesthetic. It's wise to be prepared."

Never was the "forewarned is forearmed" adage more appropriate than last spring, when I discovered I would have to be removed from my gall bladder. Friends, neighbors, and perfect strangers took it upon themselves to prepare me for this forthcoming adventure.

"I hope you don't get that horrible tube down your throat," encouraged an alto from our church choir. "My niece *still* can't pronounce her r's. . . ."

"Don't take any pills without seeing the written prescription," my sister wrote gaily from Minneapolis. "Did I ever tell you about my neighbor . . . ?"

Thanks to advice such as this, my hospital confinement was routine and predictable. I did develop a perplexing nervous tic and an irrational fear of gray metal trays—however, that's another story.

The occasional woman who is reticent about her latest disease misses out on a lot of fun. For one never knows where one may stumble across the perfect tidbit to enliven a dull afternoon. Yesterday, as I was debating the merits of stewed versus whole tomatoes at the supermarket, a voice at the other end of the store caught my attention.

"Hi, Helen!" someone shouted across Frozen Foods. "How was your hysterectomy?"

"Real fine!" Another voice—I assume it was Helen's—called

from either Imported Cheese or Ground Beef. "I was home in EIGHT DAYS!"

The woman ahead of me, picking through a pile of dented bean cans, suddenly straightened.

"Eight days?" she murmured to no one in particular. "It took me almost two weeks."

"Actually," commented an elderly nun, swerving her cart to avoid the beans, "I think they have a new technique now. My sister-in-law was telling me about it just this week. . . ."

The two of them edged casually over to Frozen Foods, and as I left the store, I noticed a rapidly growing group of shoppers in animated conversation, punctuated only by an occasional toddler falling out of his basket.

I drove home, feeling forlorn and unloved. Being excluded from the Happy Hysterectomy club can be a shattering experience. In desperation, I put away the groceries and reached for the phone.

"Hi, Barbara. Did I tell you the kids brought home a cat, and I'm allergic to it?"

"You told me last month. Have I mentioned that I'm going to have ingrown toenail surgery?"

". . . I wheezed and sneezed all night long . . ."

". . . The doctor thinks it developed because of those pointy-toed shoes . . ."

"Oh, and have you heard about Lois? Apparently, her lab tests are all back and . . ."

"Good grief," sighed my husband, and headed for the door.

He doesn't know what he's missing.

Canticle of the Car Pool

ANN

You know I hate to complain, Father, but things were a lot easier in the old days. When the children were younger, we didn't have a car. We walked wherever we went, except for some small folks perched in the stroller. Or took the bus. Or stayed home.

Times have changed, Lord. Those children have grown and we have wheels. That might be a nice combination, except that as we acquired our family chariot, our sons and daughters also acquired activities. Now I rarely have that wonderful opportunity to stay home, since nobody else does.

There's the kindergarten car pool, Father, at eleven o'clock three mornings a week. Five little people to collect and deliver home. They're awfully cute, and I enjoy their company. It's fun to eavesdrop on their conversations about classroom events. I know almost as much about Show and Tell as their teacher does. But this out-in-the-middle-of-the-morning schedule doesn't leave me much time to shop for groceries or pick up things at the cleaner's. We need some stamps from the post office, and there's a stack of overdue books waiting until I have a chance to go to the library. Still, it's worth the dashing and time-juggling to have our youngest in the parish kindergarten. Where else would he have a chance to be a palm tree in the story of Jonah and the whale?

It isn't just the school schedule that makes life difficult sometimes, Lord. That could probably be managed with a little more organization. The other children's activities have taken their toll from hours I could spend productively in my kitchen. Our Cub Scout's den meeting each Monday afternoon—it's too far for him to walk. But I did remember to thank You for inspiring someone else to volunteer as den mother this year, didn't I, even if she lives at the other end of the parish?

Then there are the teen show rehearsals every Tuesday, Thursday, and Sunday night. They last too late for the girls to walk home safely. At least we can gather up both daughters on one trip, since You so nicely arranged for them both to win roles. That too is a worthwhile activity. On opening night, the rest of the clan will add to the proud applause from the front row of the audience.

The routine stuff adds to the burden too, Father. Doctor and dentist appointments, trips to the vet for our dogs' shots, side jaunts to purchase socks and school paper. (How do they manage to use so much in such a short time?) My days are measured by miles traveled, it seems. My nights, too, since one daughter got her job at the supermarket and the other a fast-food place. I'm proud of their industry, but wish those evening shifts when they need a ride home didn't roll around so often.

Let's not even think about the state of this house, Lord. I hardly have time to look for the dust mop with all these chauffeur duties. On the rare days when nobody needs to be driven anywhere, I always seem to have a meeting I should attend myself. School board, parents' club, Scout committees, parish council—the children aren't the only ones with a full slate of activities.

It could be worse, Father. If I let the older children use the car for some of these driving chores, I still wouldn't get anything done at home. I'd be far too busy worrying about them, the fenders, city traffic, and reckless drivers. So I am content to slide behind the wheel myself a little longer. It gives me a few quiet moments alone with each child, something hard to find in a busy household.

There's another advantage I almost overlooked, Lord. With all this running around, I really treasure the few peaceful evenings to relax at home, or a day when there's no place I must go. Then I can throw myself into the laundry, vacuuming, and other cleanup chores with a grateful heart.

This hectic pace does have one more fringe benefit, doesn't it, Father? I can't recall when I last complained that my husband never takes me anywhere.

The Times of Our Lives

Happy Birthday to Me

ANN

Today is my birthday, Father. Another figure to write for the age line of personal information forms, on those few occasions when somebody wants to know something about me.

What's wrong with me, Lord? I don't mind these birthdays, marching along yearly, declaring to the world that I'm no longer a youngster. Perhaps the long memory You've given me helps. I recall those painful, becoming-an-adult years too well. I see my older children living through them now, that sweet-sad growing time. No, Father, I would never want to be a teen-ager again. They were good years, but difficult ones. Once around should be enough for anyone. Then it's time to move on.

I wouldn't want to recapture those early-married days either, Lord. Like every young wife, I thought a disagreement with my husband meant either the end of the world or the end of our marriage. I much prefer adding to the experiences we have bought by years of loving, living, and arguing together.

Young motherhood? That was a fine time too, Father. Seeing our oldest child take his first steps, speak his first words, cut his .first tooth, were moments filled with special joy. Yet I would not relive those joys at the expense of knowing him now as a young man, full of interesting thoughts and dreams he shares with me—sometimes.

I have the best of both worlds in the motherhood department now, Lord. You've given me nearly grown children to cherish as fascinating people, turning out to be fine adults. Yet there are still tiny folks at home with me all day, whose greatest delight is helping to bake cookies or splashing in the bathtub. Perhaps I'm not as fleet of foot in their pursuit as I was with their older brothers and sisters. I don't have to be. I've learned—and paid dearly for the knowledge—that little boys, quiet too long, must be checked at once. This wealth of past experience has kept many slightly flooded bathrooms from becoming indoor wading pools.

To retreat in years would mean surrendering recently made friends, who have added much to my life. Although there is great distance between us, I've kept the ties with those cherished chums of childhood too. We share special memories of our common youth and still treasure one another's friendship. Yet You have added many others to my life, people who have stretched my horizons and my interests. They are too precious to be exchanged for fewer gray hairs.

I've grown as a person, Lord, during the time past. There is so much more of the real me than could have been possible in younger days. More understanding, more compassion, more joy in life, more awareness of the beauty which abounds in this world where You have placed me. This is certainly worth acquiring at the cost of a couple of wrinkles—but let's continue to call them laugh lines.

And I've learned so much more about You, Father. You are no longer the faraway figure of my childhood, nor the constant note-taker of my teens. Now I recognize You for what You are—the Lord, the God Who has given me everything, Who sustains me in times of sorrow, Who shapes my happiness in those of joy. You have taken notice of every part of my life and share it with me. The search for a parking place when I'm late for the dentist, or my attempt to put into sensible words some idea for the parish school board, concern You. You are my Friend.

Perhaps that's the reason I'm so content with my attained years, Lord. They have been full to overflowing, filled by You. You have given me some degree of wisdom to make the most of myself over the years You offered me. Looking forward, I know that You will continue to fill my days and years with Your presence and love.

Thank You, Father, for all these years and all those which stretch unseen ahead of us. I'm eager to face them as they come— with You.

Valentines from a Family

JOAN

. . . When our six-foot-tall teen unexpectedly volunteers to take the preschooler (and her doll carriage) on a jaunt around the block . . .

. . . When the fourth-grader cleans his room without being asked, and even carries his overflowing wastebasket as far as the back door . . .

. . . When my husband phones to check the mail, and I suspect he really just wanted to talk to me . . .

. . . When I discover that my newsboy son has been placing an elderly lady's paper against her front door because "it's hard for her to walk" . . .

. . . When my bachelor brother spends his spring vacation happily escorting our kids on a magical trip to Disney World . . .

. . . When giggling, preteen girls phone and ask to speak to our shyest son . . .

. . . When the baby learns "patty-cake," identifies Grandpa, and sprouts a new tooth all in the same day . . .

. . . When my husband sternly lectures the twelve-year-old on his bike-left-in-the-driveway-again, then takes him out for a private milkshake . . .

. . . When someone plugs in the Saturday morning coffee before I've opened my eyes . . .

. . . When our extended family gets together and spends the day singing barbershop arrangements, sharing hilarious stories—and just loving one another . . .

. . . When I lift the children's Lenten mission banks, and find them heavy with coins . . .

. . . When Son Number Two spends a rainy afternoon patiently explaining the intricacies of chess to Son Number Four . . .

. . . When the faculty mails the mid-term failure notices, and none turn up in our mailbox . . .

. . . When my husband tries to look pleased about a tuna casserole supper . . .

. . . When the toddler goes potty "all by myself, Mommy!" . . .

. . . When my family prays together, and I think it means as much to them as it does to me . . .

Then I have no need for candy-filled hearts and sentimental cards. Because each day brings its own Valentine.

Remember the Rose!

JOAN

I realized during my childhood, when the doctor diagnosed my asthma as an allergy to cats, that I was not cut out to be a pet owner. My sense of frustration deepened during my early married years when even the most hardy house plants withered at my touch. As preschoolers, our children bore the stigma of being the only kids in the neighborhood whose turtles always died on the way home from the pet store. Obviously, the poor things had come in contact with me.

Being a natural Kiss of Death to any living organism used not to bother me. I honestly had no deep-down affinity for animals, being the type that would rather walk around the block than pass that frisky black dog up ahead. And although I sighed over the sprightly greenery featured in decorating magazines, there were always plastic plants available—which even *I* couldn't overwater. But basically, the desire to nourish something (other than a clutch of perpetually starving offspring) is part of every woman's nature. And so, last year, I tried again.

It all started during the summer when, quite unexpectedly, one of my rosebushes actually bloomed. My children heralded the glad tidings throughout the neighborhood, and before long friends began storming our back yard, eager to behold the miracle with their own eyes. In the midst of the champagne toasts my mother arrived, took a long look at the blossom, and offered her congratulations: "*You* grew something?" Two days later, she presented me with an ivy cutting, and as proof of her continuing trust, advised me that she would be standing by, available for midnight phone consultations.

So! I had a real house plant! And except for one crucial day when Mother felt compelled to take it home for an overnight stay in her plant Intensive Care unit, it seemed oddly contented with me.

As we settled into winter, I decided to put up some shelves in the den. We did need space for our books, but the ivy was now sporting a real vine, and I could just picture how impressively it would dangle over the volumes. While I was taking measurements, a daring thought evolved.

"Don't you think a little fish tank would look sweet on one of those shelves?" I asked my husband.

He eyed me suspiciously. "With fish in it?"

"Of course! I could put a tiny lamp on top. Indirect lighting, you know."

"*You* want to raise fish?"

"Remember the rose," I advised him.

The idea of a small fish tank did not appeal to my husband, but the idea of a big one did. On Christmas, he and the children presented me with a ten-gallon aquarium, filter system, pump, artificial plants, fluorescent lamp, colored gravel, and their prayers. The tank was too heavy to rest upon the new shelves, so I removed one of them and bought a stand for the tank. It looked beautiful, gurgling contentedly in the corner.

"Why don't we leave it like that?" the children asked hopefully, remembering years of dead turtles.

"Oh ye of little faith," I chided, herding them into the car for our trip to the pet store. "Remember the rose!"

We bought seven tropical fish as a start. "You'll need food," the pet store manager told us. "And a how-to-do-it book," his assistant mentioned helpfully. "Be sure to buy a net and an algae scraper," advised an elderly lady who had stopped in to get warm.

Our fish seemed happy in their new environment, and the shelves above the tank were a perfect place for all their supplies. I moved the ivy to a higher shelf where it could converse with our new philodendron (a congratulations gift from my son's teacher who had heard about the rose). Gradually, however, some of our finny friends developed a curious rash. I called a neighborhood teen whose aquariums were flourishing.

"Ten drops once a day," he instructed, handing me a medicine bottle. "Mrs. A., I know you grew that rose all by yourself, but you really need some help with these fish. For one thing, you should have a tank heater."

"And a thermometer," his buddy pointed out.

The pet store manager agreed. "Take some antibiotics, too," he told me. "Try changing the filter," his assistant advised, reaching for the charcoal. "Say," asked a hippie who had stopped in to buy a duck, "aren't you the lady who grew that rose?"

Depressed at having to spend that week's meat budget on fish supplies, I cheered myself by pausing at the plant counter to buy a geranium. Hopefully, the sight of it would also cheer my ivy, which had seemed a bit brown lately.

Thoroughly medicated, in water heated at a healthy temperature, two of the fish died immediately. The rest hung bravely on, gazing at me with great mournful eyes. The philodendron began to droop.

About a week later I came downstairs to find my husband thoughtfully surveying the aquarium. "You know," he sighed, "this whole corner is beginning to depress me."

I followed his glance. The fish were dancing crazily at the top of the tank, bumping into dead geranium leaves bobbing on the surface.

"All our books are still stacked in my closet," he went on quietly, "and we've spent more on this hobby than we did on the last baby."

I left him the job of dismantling the corner and wandered out to the garage. I'm not exactly good at admitting defeat. And besides, I wanted to see if there was any rose fertilizer left. After all, it's almost spring.

Beware the Ides of April

ANN

Lo, April is here. Along with buds, new grass, and the first flowers of spring, Tax Time cometh. All citizens, great and small, bear their offerings and do homage to the most powerful Internal Revenue Service.

"Render unto Caesar," my husband murmurs annually, girding for battle with the income tax return. This phrase gives the proper spiritual tone to that yearly skirmish between the Christians and the lions, soon to be shattered by his bellows of, "Where the @# $%¢&* are those *&¢%$#@ statements from the pediatrician?"

In our house, tax return time becomes an all-out search for the misplaced receipts, filed-somewhere-very-safe-but-I-can't-recall-the-place check stubs, and "Did anyone see that notebook I kept in the glove compartment to record the mileage for business and charitable trips?"

At that moment I slink away to the recesses of the basement on a business trip of my own, to fling in another load of laundry. Perhaps if his favorite old around-the-house shirt is available, he might better understand how I gave his notebook to the preschoolers when we were trapped in that traffic jam at a busy intersection. A car (our car—I'd forgotten to check the gas gauge after he took the Boy Scouts camping) stalled, tying up rush hour traffic in four directions. Anything to keep the little ones from laughing and waving to already furious motorists cursing under their collective breaths about "women drivers."

Years of matrimony have taught me that there is no proper way to offer wifely support during this panic period, except to keep fresh pots of coffee coming (is it possible to deduct $7.98 worth of ground roast from next year's return as a tax preparation expense?); hustle the children out of earshot while Daddy is making requests for information or giving his running commentary on tribal spending habits; and walk softly while carrying a jumbo-size bottle of headache remedy to the temporarily deranged.

This is the jolly season when Himself screams, "You mean that's ALL we contributed to the church?" in the tones of a severely injured Christian. (Score one for the lions.) He suffers spring memory lapse about all those Sundays he filled our offertory envelope muttering, "Lord, I don't mind Your taking it away, but couldn't You give us a little something more first?"

"Did you give anything else to charity?" he persists, ever the optimist. And I comb the recesses of my mind for possible occasions when I might have flung a dollar or two at door-to-door solicitors for flat-footed track teams. (Why do they always ring the doorbell when dinner is about to burn, or the boys are busy flooding the bathroom again? It's hard to make record book entries while sniffing the aroma of singed stew, or listening to the pitter-pat of water dripping into our entry hall from the upstairs plumbing.)

"The only good defense is a strong offense," comes to me from a son's football instruction. This, if ever, is my moment for a good defense.

"What charitable contributions did you list already, dear?" I ask in an interested, spritely manner.

"There were the regular church contributions. I've got it all down right here," he states proudly, showing me a neat page in the family ledger.

"That's lovely, dear. And it covers everything?" I question innocently.

"Of course. It's just a matter of proper organization and careful recording," he informs me.

"Even the ten dollars you gave the Cub Scouts?" I prod.

He makes a quick note and admits perhaps our charitable contributions are not as large as they should be.

"But I put down those I made at the office," he states masterfully, after a quick flurry of payroll deduction slips.

"How many trips to Cub Scout committee meetings did you make?" I query, noticing this omission from the mileage sheet.

He makes another quick note.

"How far did you drive when you took the Boy Scouts on their camp-out?" (This is beginning to be fun, I realize.)

More rapid rustling of paper and pencil.

"Did you make any calls for the church council fund drive?" I inquire helpfully.

Additional scribbling.

"Here's my list for the school board," I offer.

Since Himself also played football, he finally catches on to my strategy and launches an excellent offense of his own. He is meticulous in many areas. One of them is methodically listing expenditures in his little black book, the family ledger. This has often been quite handy in determining just how late the mortgage payment was last month, but it does have its drawbacks—which he turns against me now.

He totals all those pages. Which means, at the height of tax season, when I am wrestling with the mental picture of being sent to some jungle prison like Humphrey Bogart on the "Late Show" (why, I don't know, since we always declare everything—as our neighbors will testify, if the windows are open during our financial discussions), I am faced with an American husband's private inquisition.

"Tell me HOW you could manage to spend $83.97 at the Pants Palace in just ONE YEAR," he demands, implying that I have, tucked away somewhere in the closet, a pair of sable-lined jeans. At moments like this he ignores the fact that we have six sons who spend all their time either outgrowing or unkneeing their pants.

Since he has just scored a goal for the Christians, he can now afford to be slightly more charitable.

"Look, dear," he explains, "this little stuff is all very good. But now we have to get a firm handle on your business expenditures, since there's income to report there," in a tone that suggests the income isn't much, although the expenses are colossal.

"Here's my notebook, sweetheart," I offer. "Everything is listed —postage, car trips, office supplies. I think you have the depreciation on the typewriter and other equipment."

There's another quick shuffling of papers, as he resurrects the depreciation sheet.

"Okay. Let's drop the contribution and business angle and get down to the medical section," he proposes. "You haven't kept up the medical diary. It has no entries for November or December," he accuses me, evidence in hand.

"No one went to the doctor in November or December."

"NO ONE?" His tone indicates I've been remiss about the children's health, since EVERYONE sees the doctor frequently between Halloween and Christmas, if only out of boredom.

"The children stayed healthy this year," I explain, putting the blame for this monumental oversight squarely on our offspring.

Himself has developed a great deal of confidence in his computations (after he borrowed a neighbor's pocket calculator), but has some difficulty retaining and analyzing information.

"Are you sure those weren't corrective shoes?" he inquires about both teen daughters' prom bootery.

"Didn't the dermatologist prescribe the dishwasher for that rash on your hands?" (He forgot I didn't develop the rash until I began to worry about how we'd make the payments on the machine.)

Eventually I weary of my dual role as lion and coffee toter and throw in my lot with the Christians.

"Blessed be the poor in heart," I murmur softly, "for they shall take a standard deduction, and the short form will be their reward."

Meditation on Mother's Day

JOAN

Giving birth does not complete the maternal process, I've discovered. There are exquisite subtleties which must be experienced before one can truly achieve this status.

You'll know you're becoming a real mother when:

You realize suddenly that there's nothing more satisfying than a newborn asleep on your shoulder.

Rubber duckies and rag dolls nestle alongside your pots and pans.

At a dinner party, you automatically cut the meat of the stranger sitting next to you.

You look at the innocence on a small sleeping face and hear yourself whispering, "Lord, take care of her."

Indelibly imprinted on your brain is the quickest route to the pediatrician's office.

Your husband mentions that you're murmuring, "Look, Jimmy, look. See Spot run," in your sleep.

You fracture your big toe while demonstrating the proper way to steer a two-wheeled bike.

You watch the excitement in a First Communicant's eyes and hear yourself whispering, "Lord, take care of him."

Your recipe inventory consists of six two-ingredient budget casseroles, and twenty-nine variations on chocolate chip cookies.

You can reel off the names of the seven dwarfs in five seconds flat.

An exciting Sunday afternoon involves a trip to the zoo, three back-seat fistfights, and dinner at a roadside hamburger haven.

In front of the mirror, you rehearse ten good reasons why the kids cannot have a myna bird.

Your husband gets his business messages written on comic book margins in yellow crayon.

You watch the self-conscious grin on the face of an eighth-grade graduate and hear yourself whispering, "Lord, take care of him."

You can identify any Top 40 rock tune in five seconds flat.

Calm family discussions concerning the state of the union and the proper length of a parish council term are replaced by ear-splitting family discussions concerning the state of a certain bedroom, and the proper length of teen-age hair.

You find yourself visiting the supermarket at eight-hour intervals.

Your elderly neighbor mentions that your high-schoolers have been shoveling her walk all winter, and you didn't even know.

You can't decide which is worse—car-pooling, or handing over the keys.

You send the kids off to college with giant bags of dimes, for hamburgers, coin-operated laundries—and toll calls home.

You turn on "Sesame Street" because it's too quiet to concentrate and insist that your youngest host a marathon sleep-in.

You watch the joyous smile on the face of a radiant bride and hear yourself whispering, "Lord, take care of her."

You realize suddenly that there's nothing more satisfying than a newborn asleep on your shoulder.

A happy Mother's Day to women of all ages, sizes, and states of mind. How truly blessed we are!

The Good Ole Summertime

JOAN

Ah, summertime! With carefree lazy days to sop up the sun, picnic in the yard, lounge in casual comfort. At least, that's what
I've always heard. At our house, however . . .

6:00 A.M. Three-year-old in bed with us. Demands cereal. Two
teen-age sons telling jokes in kitchen. Will leave for jobs at caddy
shack as soon as gang arrives. Radio rock station top volume.

Caddy gang arrives. All tell jokes in kitchen. Loud guffaws. One
broken dish.

Caddies leave. Phone rings. Customer wishes newspaper. Newsboy son still in sleeping bag on neighbor's patio. Wake Newsboy.
Also wake neighbor's dog.

Three-year-old demands egg. Turn on TV. Wake Husband.
Clean up kitchen. Dress. Three-year-old demands waffle. Newsboy
returns from route, goes back to bed. Husband eats. Wake eight-
year-old for swim class. Phone rings. Customer has missed paper.
Wake Newsboy again. Clean up kitchen.

Eight-year-old's gerbils loose. Eight-year-old at swim class. Lock
gerbils in bathroom; take three-year-old to neighbor's bathroom.

Throw in first load laundry. Newsboy's friends at back door. Wake Newsboy.

Clothes drier not working. Hang jeans in yard. Fill wading pool for three-year-old and friends. Break up water fight. Rehang jeans far end of yard.

Eight-year-old swimmer returns. Gerbils rescued. Large stray dog at back door. Three-year-old screaming. Answer phone. Turn off rock music. Turn off TV. Clean up kitchen. Swimmer's friends at back door. All go upstairs.

Vacuum living room. Make beds. Swimmer wishes lemonade stand. Swimmer has tantrum. Friends banished. Answer phone. Turn off rock music. Hang second load jeans. Clean kitchen in time for lunch.

Husband home for lunch. Suggests picnic. Husband to McDonald's for lunch.

Caddy Number Two returns. No job today. Caddy eats. Will cut lawn. Three-year-old and friends wish snack. Hang third load clothes. Answer phone. Clean up kitchen. Stray dog has eaten three-year-old's snack. Three-year-old screaming.

Swimmer goes to pool. Newsboy returns from pool. Eats lunch. Will clean room.

Swimmer returns from pool. Caddy goes to pool. Will cut grass later. Clean up kitchen. List groceries for Sunday picnic. Make three phone calls for committee chairwoman. No one answers. Bake cake for tomorrow's birthday boy. Wrap gift. Hide gift. Fill wading pool again for three-year-old. Confiscate firecrackers from Swimmer.

Newsboy goes to park. Will clean room later. Husband phones. Office air conditioner broken. Has had hard day. Husband disconnected.

Clean kitchen for dinner. Rewrap gift. Banish three-year-old to sandbox. Caddy returns. Will definitely cut grass. Empties wading pool on three-year-old. Three-year-old screaming. Clean up wet sand from picnic table. Iron one shirt.

Newsboy returns from park. Split lip. Apply ice. Gerbil has bitten Swimmer's friend. Swimmer's friend's mother irate. Apply ice. Look up insurance policy. Answer phone. Turn off TV.

Caddy Number One returns. Picks up golf clubs. Will be late for dinner. Caddy Number Two finishes lawn. Eats early dinner, has meeting. Newsboy feels faint. Cannot clean room. Cleans room.

Swimmer, Newsboy, three-year-old eat dinner. Clean up kitchen. Newsboy cannot help. Feels faint. Newsboy's friends at back door for baseball game. Newsboy leaves with mitt.

Confiscate more firecrackers from Swimmer. Swimmer to pool. Bath for three-year-old. Three-year-old waterlogged. Answer phone. Newsboy needs snack. Three-year-old in bed. Hang fourth load laundry.

Husband home for dinner. Serve Husband. Swimmer home from pool. Frisk Swimmer. Swimmer needs snack. Will clean up family room first. Swimmer has tantrum, is sent to bed. Answer phone. Clean up family room.

Caddy Number One returns. Eats dinner, reviews phone messages. Turn off rock station. Clean up kitchen. Newsboy returns. Needs snack. Caddy Number Two returns. Needs snack. Make three phone calls for committee chairwoman. No one answers. Clean up kitchen. Swimmer needs snack. Spank Swimmer, send back to bed. Caddy Number Two playing piano. Iron second shirt.

Husband irate. Cannot have peace in own home. Merely matter of proper organization. Three-year-old screaming. Swimmer and Newsboy fighting. Piano playing. Phone ringing. TV blaring. Caddy gang at door. Raining on fourth laundry load. Husband needs snack.

Pick up purse and bottle of cola. Locate car keys and yesterday's newspaper. Leave house. Insert key in ignition. Back out of driveway over wading pool.

Drive to shopping center parking lot under lamppost. Read newspaper. Drink cola. Smoke cigarette. Count days till school starts. Listen to silence. Enjoy summer.

For Whom Does the
School Bell Toll?

ANN

It's been quite a summer. The back door never went ten minutes without a bang, heralding someone coming in for something, or someone going out with something someone else would come in to look for just a few minutes later.

It's been hot months of late dinners because of softball practice, early dinners to accommodate softball games, and dinners in shifts for those going out to or coming home from work. How often dinner was cold cuts and potato salad served on paper plates when "It's not my turn for the dishes tonight!" discussions were more than hot parents could bear.

It's been sand, sand everywhere, a wall-to-wall carpeting of grit and heat-shed dog hair. Shoes removed from small feet just before bath time supplied the upstairs floor covering. That downstairs was more efficiently brought in with pails and shovels and small plastic cars that had been entombed in the sandbox overnight.

It's been dogs and weeds in the garden, children under the hose in their best clothes, shoes misplaced and needed to convey little feet over the hot boards on the back porch. When shoes couldn't be found, Mother had to do the conveying, then return a few minutes later to carry another would-be door-banger in for a new supply of things to bring out.

It's been wet bathing suits left in the bathroom, then searched for unsuccessfully in dresser drawers. It's been fights by three children over four nose plugs, only two of which can be found at any one time.

It's been sunburn, mosquito bites, and dehydration that will yield only to another pitcher of lemonade, but who took the sugar?

It's been teen-age daughters courting a lovely tan, stretched out on the very best sheets in the yard, while the phone rang incessantly.

It's been weeding and watering the parched garden, shampooing and scrubbing small bodies fresh from the sandbox, constant sweeping, and perpetual laundering of sprinkler-sodden clothes.

It's been extra ten-year-olds for lunch, surplus teens for dinner, and "Let's all run down for a swim!" when dishwashing time rolled around.

It's been arguments over unmade beds, unwashed dishes, undumped trash, followed by, "Please, can't we go out after dinner? We worked so hard today!"

It's been early July thumbing of catalogues for school clothes, fervent maternal prayers that summer would soon be over, with the traffic headed out in the morning once again, not to return until late afternoon.

Now the time has come. Crisp new clothes are hanging in the closets. Notebooks and pencils have been unearthed from safe keeping places. The alarm clock is set for early morning on the first day of school.

Another summer is over. Everyone survived—somehow. But now I realize how much I will miss the noise, the ever-present company with a glass stretched out for cold juice and assorted hands reaching constantly for cookies.

Another school year has come. Another daughter leaves high school behind for the challenge of college. Another son takes his place in the full-time world of first grade. Ahead lie months of quiet, peace unbroken by banging doors, dripping children, dogs in the tomatoes.

Another year to carry children further from boisterous summer living toward the quiet fall of adulthood. Another year closer to a house empty of children.

But God, in His Goodness, has arranged that there will still be summers with children small enough to find fascination in watching ants, capturing caterpillars, gathering dandelions for Mom. And children of all ages who find delight in turning the hose on brothers and sisters who aren't looking in their direction.

Stan Laurel and Me

JOAN

It all started quite innocently during the waning days of summer
vacation.

"There's a box of old clothes in the garage," said Number
Three Son one morning. "Can we use some?"

I agreed, glad for a respite from the usual "what-can-we-do-now-
Mom?" An hour later, I glanced out the window into an unusually quiet yard where boys of all sizes and shapes sat shredding
and folding newspapers. Two of my sons and Jeff-from-down-the-
street seemed to be in command, but all were busily engaged in
something.

"Hey, Mom," shouted Number Two, "can we borrow your
head?"

"My what?"

"You know—your wig stand."

I should live so long. "Of course not."

Several hours later, the crew pounded on the back door, eager
to show off their project. I had to admit it was impressive—a full-
sized dummy, stuffed with wood and paper, and dressed rummage-
sale style. A local beauty shop, I later learned, had supplied its

wig-stand head, which now sported features slightly reminiscent of Stan Laurel.

"What are you going to do with it—him?" I asked in fascination.

"Probably use him for tackle practice during football season," ventured Jeff-from-down-the-street.

School began a short time later, and Mr. Dummy, along with a half-finished companion begun over the Labor Day weekend, languished in the garage, used only for sporadic football workouts. I assumed the project, like so many other childhood ventures, was slowly dying from disinterest.

But I was wrong. A few weeks later I entered the garage to find Dummy Number Two, dressed in raggy denim and sporting a Chicago Cub hat, perched jauntily on the seat of my bike. Stan Laurel lounged drunkenly against the picnic table, surveying the scenery with interest.

"I thought you guys had gone out of the dummy business," I asked the kids that evening. They shrugged (which is their usual form of communication).

During the next few weeks, the dummy population increased. Like uninvited guests they crept over the nooks and crannies of our already bulging house. A half-finished leg on the dining room table; two heads in the bathtub; Oliver Hardy, Jr., dressed in an aging Lord Fauntleroy suit, posing prettily on the front steps. I once curiously surveyed a strange-looking cowboy who sat quietly on the neighbor's patio all afternoon, before realizing it was another of our creations.

Jeff-from-down-the-street's mother was not exempt from this merrymaking, for when we eventually ran out of space, the headquarters moved to her house. The children spent many happy hours in her garage fashioning more playmates, but the day she entered her empty living room to find two dummies watching "Gilligan's Island" reruns, she put her placid foot down.

"Kids," she decreed, "either *do* something with these dummies, or get rid of them."

Her ultimatum, however, produced only a more frantic outburst of labor among the boys, who were by now raiding dresser drawers and neighborhood woodpiles for material to support their habit.

On Halloween afternoon, I dressed the toddler in her "Little Devil" costume and helped with the boys' make-up.

"Are you going trick-or-treating down at Jeff's house?" Number Two asked, a little too casually.

"I suppose so," I answered. "Why?"

"Nothin'," he murmured. But as Daughter and I began our rounds, I sensed that something definitely unusual was Going On down the street.

Mothers stood in small clusters, gesturing, laughing, and shaking their heads. Children whooped and pointed. Cars passing me slowed to a crawl at mid-block, obviously surveying something I could not yet see.

It had to be faced. Grasping Daughter's hand, I made my way through the spectators to Jeff's house.

The sight was truly awe inspiring. Dummies in various stages of Halloween mayhem dangled from trees, windows, and the roof. Stan Laurel posed on a dormer, threatening a silent opponent with a rubber hatchet. A goblin-like figure lay vanquished on the lawn. Two villains engaged in mortal combat by the chimney, spotlighted in the approaching dusk by the bulb of a flashlight game which had mysteriously disappeared from our closet. Capping the splendor were eerie moans and laments coming from a loudspeaker, and sounding suspiciously like some very familiar children.

Jeff's mother wandered to the door, looking unusually haggard. "Don't ask how they got on the roof," she said.

"The moans and groans?"

"I rewind the tape recorder every hour."

A neighbor stared at the roof in fascination.

"So that's where David's First Communion suit went," she murmured.

All good things must eventually end, and with the advent of winter, the children's dummy mania has waned. But I suspect the subject is not yet finished, for I happened to overhear Number Three's telephone conversation with Jeff last night.

"Next year," he was saying, "let's do it at our house. . . ."

A Perfect Holiday Meal

ANN

Piles of cookbooks topple over in my kitchen. They're full of exotic recipes for marinated kumquats and stuffed zucchini. But I'm still searching for one written in the takes-nothing-for-granted spirit of the old-fashioned cookbook that began its recipe for rabbit stew, "First catch one rabbit. . . ." To survive Thanksgiving, I really need some kind of scheduling guide, the sort that helps a bride and groom arrange each wedding detail at the proper time. The best day-by-day, week-by-week checklist of things to do would have to include:

FIRST WEEK IN NOVEMBER: Lie down until urge to invite whole clan for Thanksgiving passes, or sister-in-law offers to do it, whichever comes first.

SECOND WEEK IN NOVEMBER: If neither item listed for last week successful, invite whole clan for Thanksgiving. Take positive approach to occasion. Vow *this year* will be fun, elegant, properly organized. Forget all previous disasters.

Check out suitable serving platters, dishes, casseroles, compotes, etc. Dig only good linen tablecloth out of bottom of ironing basket. Iron tablecloth. Polish silver. Take stock of china, crystal. Plan to sterilize dog's dish for Uncle Mortimer, who's a little farsighted so won't notice his plate doesn't match rest of crockery. Empty three jars of jelly into compotes to finish out necessary number of matching glasses for festive gathering. Borrow three more compotes from neighbors.

Try to remember why having whole family together for Thanksgiving seemed like good idea. Sit down and cry.

THIRD WEEK IN NOVEMBER: Time to get down to serious business. Ask husband for more grocery money. Make pointed mention of his brother's appetite. Listen to husband complain about your relatives' ability to inhale huge quantities of food whenever somebody else foots bill. Sit down and cry. Collect extra grocery money from penitent husband.

Arrange kindergartner's turkey drawn around hand on paper plate in suitable display on refrigerator door. Place second-grader's papier-mâché pilgrims on top of china cabinet. Make room on coffee table for sixth-grader's reconstruction of *Mayflower* landing at Plymouth Rock. Wallop dog for eating poop deck of *Mayflower*.

Move everything to dust.

FOURTH WEEK IN NOVEMBER: Detailed scheduling now critical. Compose lists of tasks for each day.

MONDAY: Call sister-in-law. Ask her to make fancy gelatin mold. Sister-in-law says too busy, doesn't have time. Inquire whether sister-in-law's children ever had chicken pox. Mention funny rash on your children. Accept sister-in-law's regrets when she suddenly remembers previous holiday dinner date at her mother's.

TUESDAY: Make complete shopping list. Add hot dogs and large bag of charcoal for possible emergency weenie roast. Prepare to cope with repeat of year forgot to remove plastic bag of turkey innards before cooking and turkey exploded all over kitchen.

Calculate amount of stale bread still needed for turkey stuffing. Stop cautioning children to close bread wrappers after making sandwiches. Hunt for favorite turkey stuffing recipe used as bookmark somewhere in garden catalogue last spring. Order two extra bottles of cooking sherry for Aunt Martha, who never touches hard stuff.

Be firm when refusing Cousin Tillie's request to bring friend who doesn't want to be alone for Thanksgiving. Borrow three folding tables, ten chairs, and piano bench to seat Cousin Tillie's friend, husband, six children, bachelor uncle, and three out-of-town visitors who would have been alone.

Go to store to do complete shopping. Unpack groceries. Sit down and cry. Return to store. Buy turkey.

WEDNESDAY: Begin to bake pumpkin pies. Stop baking pies. Help dog deliver six puppies under kitchen table. Chase thirteen strange children out of kitchen. Finish baking pies.

Cook and mash turnips. Ignore cries of "Yuch!" and "Do we have to *eat* that junk?" from offspring. Prepare other vegetables, stuffing, salad. Put in refrigerator. Slap seven familiar hands reaching for carrot sticks.

Go to bed early with sick headache. Get up at midnight to put forgotten turkey out to thaw.

THURSDAY: Add oysters to stuffing. Remember Aunt Hildegarde allergic to oysters. Fish oysters out of stuffing. Stuff turkey. Light oven. Notice funny smell. Remove four-year-old's plastic dinosaur from oven. Roast turkey. Air kitchen.

Arrange good tablecloth on table. Set table. Check turkey. Hear crash. Remove toddler from table. Spank toddler. Sweep up broken glass. Send ten-year-old next door to borrow jar of jelly and compote dish. Empty jelly into dish. Wash jar and place on table.

Bathe and dress children. Move dog and puppies to basement. Tell protesting children just heard tornado alert on radio. Take silver serving dishes out of hiding. Repolish tarnished dishes.

Remove china and cloth from table over which husband now hanging new chandelier hasn't had time to get to for six months. Scream at husband. Sit down and cry. Wash china. Iron clean sheet to use for tablecloth.

Sterilize dog's dish for Uncle Mortimer. Cook giblets for gravy. Burn giblets for gravy. Feed giblets to dog. Make gravy with large lumps of flour everyone supposed to think are giblets. Give quick rinse to dog's dish. Remind self Uncle Mortimer convinced germs exist only in sick minds. Reset table.

Shower. Dress. Children too quiet. Look for children. Discover filthy children playing in basement with dog and puppies. Sit down and cry. Give children light dusting.

Doorbell rings. Answer door. Greet guests. Promise self to have wonderful time. Start by reminding sister-in-law this year her turn to hostess Christmas.

Some Last-minute Suggestions for Santa

JOAN

Something's definitely wrong. I've done the shopping, wrapped and hidden presents (hope I can remember where the thirty-gallon aquarium is stashed), and mailed cards. The house, if not exactly *gracious*, is at least tinsel-decked and fumigated, with holly hiding the no-longer-scrubbable fingerprints on banisters and door-jambs. No one has discovered my cache of decorated cookies, and the tree is still upright (surrounding it with wire mesh this year was a clever touch). Within an hour, most of us will be leaving for Midnight Mass, where the choir's jubilant "Alleluia!" will echo our own, filling our souls with the peace of this most beautiful season.

And yet I have forgotten something. It nags me as I sit here in the candles' glow, relaxed and (unbelievably) ALONE for a few moments. What have I overlooked?

Of course. My annual letter to Santa Claus. I've always felt that mothers, too, have a right to communicate with this jolly old fellow, if only to clarify their offsprings' lists. (Ignore Number Two, Santa, we really don't need a baby elephant.)

But perhaps it isn't too late. Even though you're already start-ing your rounds, Santa, I'll send my thoughts across the heavens to you. For I have a wish list too, with items just a bit different from the usual requests.

You and I both know that gifts of the spirit are infinitely more precious (and longer-lasting) than those wrapped in foil paper and destined to be broken before tomorrow's turkey is served. So this year I ask you for some of life's intangibles, for others as well as myself.

Bring my parents continued good health, Santa, and maintain their cheerful, supportive dispositions. How much a part of every holiday they have been, and how grateful we are that they can still share our lives so abundantly. When words fail us, as they so often do, touch these dear grandparents' hearts with our unspoken message of gratitude and love. And send our special wishes to an-other set of parents too, Santa, who already live the eternal Christmas we will one day share.

For my teen-agers, I ask courage and wisdom, the strength to be their own people in a follow-the-crowd world. Calm their some-times confused souls, their worries over dates and driving and chemistry tests and nagging mothers. Hold tightly to their hands as they approach the precipice of adulthood, Santa, and reassure them that the best is definitely yet to be.

For my precious middle child, I wish the knowledge that he is truly appreciated. How often he is overlooked in a household so long dominated by rock albums and high chairs. And yet he goes comfortably along, a calm presence in the midst of the usual chaos. Maintain his easy disposition, Santa, and assure him that his value to us can never be measured in human terms.

And the youngest pair—you know as well as I do that they could benefit from a large package of patience (or is it their mother who has most need of this virtue?). Bring my little ones all good things—kindness, generosity, and that wide-eyed sense of wonder that makes the universe their own personal treasure chest. And perhaps, just perhaps, the need to fall asleep by eight o'clock each evening.

I haven't forgotten my husband, Santa, the man I learned to

love so long ago. Together we have forged this life, like two phoenixes rising again and again out of the ashes of despair into a rekindled hope for tomorrow. Fill my beloved spouse with understanding and acceptance of his so-often-confusing routine, grant him continued fortitude as he struggles to guide and protect those entrusted to his care. Fill him with peace of soul as he continues in this labor of love.

And then there's me, Santa, the glue that holds this dear family together. I could ask you for a multitude of gifts, all designed to make my life easier and more rewarding. But instead, I wish only for mercy. Mercy for those who try my patience and fall short of my expectations. And mercy for myself too, that I accept me as I am, with all my foibles, impossible habits, and frustrating limitations. If only I can one day learn to be as tolerant of myself as I try to be of others.

Most important, on this very special evening and throughout the coming years, let our family remember the blessing that is really Christmas—the coming of the Child. Pull us away from our concern with material wishes, and guide us toward Him Who patiently waits to share the joy and sorrow of this life, and the promise of the next.

So as you begin your midnight journey, Santa, remember the presents most needed at our home. We will, of course, be happy with anything you bring. But nothing will glitter as brightly under our tree as these special treasures, gifts of our spirit, the jewels of our love.

Confessions of a Contented Woman

ANN

"How can you possibly be fulfilled?" she asked me, Lord—this old friend I hadn't seen since college.

When we parted so many years ago, we chose different paths to the end of the rainbow. Many things have happened since then, Lord, that I couldn't explain to her.

How could I say that I chose to join my life to that of the man who is the center of my world, and I of his? How could I tell her, Father, that love, contentment, and friendship have grown ever stronger, as we rejoiced and sorrowed together, as we have become closer over the years? How could I explain that the dreams we dreamed so long ago were only shadows of the happiness in our life?

How could I make her understand, Father, that I live with him, not through him? That I love him so much, his triumphs delight me more than my own? That his greatest pleasure is in what I accomplish, not what he achieves?

How could I tell her the thrill of a small warm hand in mine, that of a tiny son who trusts me completely? And that these little people have taught me to place my own hand in Yours, trusting You with the same childlike faith?

How could I describe for her the sounds of Love? The enthusiastic banging of a crib, as a just-learned-to-stand-up baby catches sight of his father and crows, "Da-da!" as though Christmas had come? Or the seldom-heard, "What do you think, Mom?" when a teen daughter tries to choose a special dress? Is it possible to share these sounds of love, which can be heard only in the heart of a parent?

How could I tell her that raising this family has challenged me to the fullest in mind, body, heart, and soul? That I have grown to meet the challenge and embrace it joyfully?

How could I explain that I am my own person, freely committed to those most dear to me in this world? That I am irreplaceable in their hearts and their home? Or that I have the greatest freedom, that which is within me to be given to others?

How could she know that I am rich in all things but those of this world? That the treasures of my heart are overflowing beyond my dreams?

How could I tell her what it is like to live in an atmosphere of love? Or that the clean socks, well-done homework papers, and sometimes-washed-without-nagging dishes are each day's valentines?

How could I describe, Father, the satisfaction in a job nearly done, as I see three teens well on their way to Christian maturity? And knowing that I have played a major part in their formation as persons?

How could I express the delight of three medium-sized boys who rush home from school, eager to share with Mom the little triumphs and tragedies of their day?

How could I tell her the way it feels to share some very special days—the first day of kindergarten, grammar school graduation, a senior prom, then off to college? And to have earned a place in them by living countless "ordinary" days which have brought these loved, loving children to such milestones?

How could I describe the warmth that comes when I hear a child, preschool or high school, state confidently, "Mom can do anything!" and mean it? Or the happiness I find in the cheerful announcement, "I'm home, Mom!"?

How could she imagine that these sons and daughters, which You have given to us in trust, are a living tribute to the love and devotion of two chosen people?

How could she know, Father, that my rainbow has so many exquisite colors? Or that, at the end of it, I have found my gold?